INTERNATIONAL AGRICULTURAL LIBRARIANSHIP

INTERNATIONAL AGRICULTURAL LIBRARIANSHIP

CONTINUITY AND CHANGE

Proceedings of An
International Symposium Held
at the National Agricultural Library
November 4, 1977

Edited by ALAN FUSONIE
and LEILA MORAN

Sponsored by the Associates of the National Agricultural
Library, Inc. and the National Agricultural Library

GREENWOOD PRESS
WESTPORT, CONNECTICUT • LONDON, ENGLAND

Library of Congress Cataloging in Publication Data
Main entry under title:

International agricultural librarianship.

Includes index.
1. Agricultural libraries—Congresses. 2. Inter-
national librarianship—Congresses. 3. Agriculture—
Information services—International cooperation—
Congresses. I. Fusonie, Alan. II. Moran, Leila
Padgett, 1924-   III. United States. National
Agricultural Library. Associates. IV. United States.
National Agricultural Library.
Z675.A83I57   026'.63   78-67916
ISBN 0-313-20640-6

Z
675
A83
I57

Library of Congress Catalog Card Number: 78-67916
ISBN: 0-313-20640-6

First published in 1979

Greenwood Press, Inc.
51 Riverside Avenue, Westport, Connecticut 06880

Printed in the United States of America

10 9 8 7 6 5 4 3 2 1

Contents

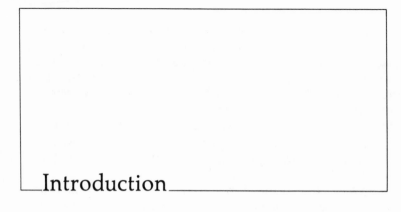

Introduction

Today, the food-producing countries are being asked to share their abundance with the millions of hungry people in the world. Factors vital to the future of the world food supply include the following: less costly farm machinery; development of indigenous farm machinery for less developed countries; development of alternative sources of energy; increased input into basic research; improvements in more and better high-yielding crop strains; more effective land use; a worldwide agricultural meteorological network; and a world food reserve system. These represent only a sampling of the many basic challenges facing the world agricultural community.

There is a growing consensus that food may be one of the most complex economic, political, and moral issues of our time. In this regard, agricultural librarians, documentalists, and information specialists have a vital role to play in providing timely and relevant informational services to the many farmers, livestock producers, agribusiness organizations, research workers, subject specialists, teachers, students, and others who are actively engaged in meeting the continuing challenge of man, food, and hunger.

The idea for a symposium which would focus attention upon the practical role of agricultural librarians, documentalists, and

information specialists, and their growing importance in terms
of informational services to the world community, was formulated in the spring of 1977. It was decided that the symposium
would be highlighted by a special tribute to Foster Mohrhardt,
former director of the National Agricultural Library, who,
among other accomplishments, is a former president of the following organizations: the Association of Research Libraries;
the American Library Association; the International Association of Agricultural Librarians and Documentalists; and the U.S.
Book Exchange.

By May of the same year, with the theme defined and the
suggested papers lined up, the identification of potential audiences, sponsorship, publicity, and the development of an attractive registration brochure were under way. As the program
became more formalized, Greenwood Press, Inc., of Westport,
Connecticut, agreed to publish the edited proceedings.

The one-day symposium, which was held on November 4,
1977, was not only informative and interesting but also steeped
with enthusiasm, nostalgia, and good friendship. It was attended
by over one hundred registrants, of whom over half were either
university- or government-affiliated. The presentations at this
meeting included introductory remarks, major papers, oral
panel discussions, and closing remarks (an epilogue). Participants
included agricultural librarians, directors of libraries, the Archivist of the United States, agricultural historians, information
scientists, and others. In addition, the following exhibits added
a fitting dimension: the Oberly Award; Food and Nutrition
Division of the Special Libraries Association; Oryx Press;
AGRIS; Greenwood Press; Associates of the National Agricultural Library, Inc.; the Hollinger Corporation; and the National
Agricultural Library. A special debt of thanks is owed to the
Hamby Company of Plainview, Texas, for the generous dona-
tion of their relevant bumper sticker, "If you eat, you are involved in agriculture."

The symposium produced not only a memorable day but
also this volume of useful educational documents in the area
of agricultural librarianship and documentation. Because of
the international and interdisciplinary nature of the symposium,

the diverse styles of references were in some instances left as submitted since they reflect the intent and integrity of the originators. The texts of all papers have been slightly revised.

Special thanks should be given to the panelists Carol Alexander, David Lee, Gerry Ogden, and Wayne Rasmussen, to Judy Ho for organizing the exhibits, to Jayne MacLaine for arranging the superb luncheon and dinner, to Irene Glennon for her time and effort in preparing the index to these proceedings, and to Richard Farley, director of the National Agricultural Library, for his advice and unstinting support. Finally, appreciation should be extended to Donna Jean Fusonie for her outstanding editorial assistance in reviewing the manuscript every step of the way.

Alan Fusonie
Leila Moran

INTERNATIONAL
AGRICULTURAL
LIBRARIANSHIP

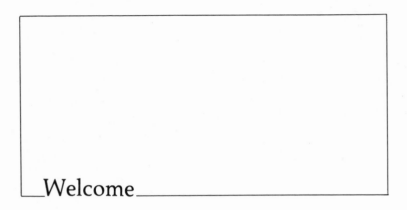

Welcome

Today's symposium is in honor of our good friend and colleague Foster E. Mohrhardt who over the years has contributed in so many ways to the development of international agricultural librarianship and documentation. We are deeply grateful and fortunate that Foster was persuaded to give a paper on this special occasion.

As an educational document, the published proceedings will hopefully represent a meaningful contribution toward the advancement of the importance of agricultural librarianship and documentation to the agricultural and/or world community.

On behalf of Secretary Bergland and the staff of the National Agricultural Library, I welcome you and assure you that we will do our best to make your brief stay with us productive, profitable, and pleasant.

Richard A. Farley, Director
National Agricultural Library
U.S. Department of Agriculture
Beltsville, Maryland

The Changing Nature of Agricultural Librarianship: Observations and Overview

*J. RICHARD BLANCHARD**

I suppose a scholarly study of agricultural librarianship should begin with the eighteenth century with the establishment of the agricultural and horticultural society libraries of Europe and the United States. Instead, I prefer to present the subject from a personal point of view as I have observed it since the year 1947—thirty years ago. That was the year Ralph Shaw at the U.S. Department of Agriculture (USDA) gave me a job in his library. Previously, I had spent a few years at the Library of Congress and had undergone a stint in the Navy during World War II. In fact, I was still in uniform when Ralph first interviewed me. I remember him saying that although I was a navy type he might be able to use my services. He would, he said, give me a trial period of six weeks as chief of the Reference Department. If my work was satisfactory, I could remain as chief. If not, *other* arrangements would be made.

This all sounded rather ominous but I decided to take the position. I started work at the USDA Library during the first hot spell of the summer. Several strong impressions remain of my experiences that year—the overwhelmingly institutional aspect of the library's quarters in the old South Building, the

*J. Richard Blanchard is Librarian Emeritus, University of California, Davis.

awful sticky heat of Washington before air conditioning was generally available, the harried and almost frenetic air of the staff, and the great pressure of work. But most of all I remember the people—the dynamic, gimlet-eyed Ralph Shaw, greatly feared and respected, Louise Bercaw, his assistant, wise and gracious, and a corps of efficient librarians—Margaret Bryant, Pauline Jennings, Bella Shachtman, Ruby Moats, Angelina Carabelli, Oliver Shipley, Wilma Frances, and others. On the surface it was a very conventional library, but one sensed a dynamism beneath the surface. Some changes had occurred and others were on the way—pushed along by the brilliant and restless Shaw chafing under the dead weight of a huge bureaucracy and striving to introduce significant and pioneering innovations which would improve procedures and services.

I did survive the trial period and continued in charge of reference services. In 1949, I changed jobs, moving to the University of Nebraska as librarian of the College of Agriculture, and in 1951, I went to the Library of the University of California at Davis, where I remained. The college libraries, with their more placid atmosphere, were very different from the government library, but they too were on the brink of great growth and change. It was an exciting time—the late 1940s and early 1950s. Old practices lingered on, but dreams and experimentation were in the air. We were hopeful and we had energy. Now, in 1977, many of our dreams have been fulfilled and further change is coming fast, but ironically, we are not so hopeful.

Perhaps the best way to review these changes is in the library school textbook manner, starting with administration and proceeding through the various aspects of technical and public services, comparing practices in government and academic libraries in the 1940s and 1950s with procedures in the late 1970s.

ADMINISTRATIVE PRACTICES

Libraries in the 1940s were beginning to reflect changes in the administrative practices initiated years before by industry

which were based on the scientific management movement
formulated by Frederick W. Taylor.[1] Taylor's principles involved the systematic observation and classification of job
activities as they were carried out, and then the simplification
of the task to be done based on an analysis of motion, material,
and equipment. Frank and Lillian Gilbreth (*Cheaper by the
Dozen*) extended Taylor's concepts and popularized them. Other
movements also had an impact. For instance, the industrial
psychology movement and the human relations movement gave
more emphasis to the psychological aspects of personnel utilization as compared to emphasis on the physical aspects by Taylor.

Because of efforts by the federal civil service system, government libraries in many instances instituted work rationalization
and job analysis methods sooner than academic and public
libraries. At the USDA Library in 1947, for instance, we care-
fully compiled job descriptions and did thorough workflow
studies using forms supplied by the Civil Service Commission or
the Bureau of the Budget.[2] But such procedures were not
adopted at many academic and public libraries until much later.
On the other hand, in the USDA Library of 1947 the boss was
still the boss. Shaw had regular meetings of the staff and information was exchanged, but one didn't often question the chief
or argue much about his decisions. In this respect Shaw was,
oddly enough, rather old-fashioned. I found the academic libraries at the time more relaxed in this respect with greater participation by the staff in decision-making. With the years there has
been an equalization process. Academic libraries now use work
rationalization procedures as a matter of course—often in con-
nection with automation—and full staff participation must now
be part of the administrative process in any government library.
This process certainly became very evident during Foster Mohrhardt's enlightened administration of the National Agricultural
Library (NAL) and has obviously been carried on by Richard
Farley whose previous experience has been in academic institutions.

Efforts to centralize library services required as much attention in the 1940s as it does today. One of Shaw's most brilliant
coups was to persuade the Secretary of Agriculture that the in-

dividual bureau libraries of the Department of Agriculture
should be merged administratively and, in most cases, physically
with the central USDA Library. This was done in 1942 in the
face of much resistance by the Bureaus. According to a ques-
tionnaire sent out in 1947, twenty-five out of forty land-grant
colleges maintained departmental libraries,[3] some under the
jurisdiction of the librarians and others under deans or departmental chairmen. The struggle to centralize continues today
in academic institutions. In recent years, some progress has
been made with the merger of small units and the shifting of
administrative responsibility to the head librarians. Often
these changes have occurred not because faculty members
have had a change of heart but, rather, because colleges were
financially unable to support so many units with the resultant
duplication in costs. The desire to have small basic collections
close at hand remains. For some scientists this is an entirely
legitimate need and librarians should not ignore it. In this respect, in the eyes of some of our clientele, library services
may have deteriorated in recent years.

A great administrative difficulty in 1947 involved obtaining
qualified librarians. They were scarce and remained in short
supply until the 1960s. Some government libraries had only a
few professionals in 1947, and many of the administrative and
technical people had gained expertise on the job; this was particularly true of the Library of Congress at the time. But, in
general, it seemed to me that the staffs were very dedicated.
The old work ethic remained. The depression had not been
forgotten. Now there is an adequate, indeed an oversupply of
librarians, but the work ethic may have become frayed over
the years. There is perhaps more theoretical expertise in libraries now, but I doubt that personal productivity has increased. On the other hand, automation in some cases has
more than made up the difference. So we have a mixed bag.
Not everything is rosy now as far as library administrative
and personnel practices are concerned, but progress has certainly been made. Our staffs are more involved; many in-
equities concerning race and sex have been alleviated; and,
in general, we are doing a better job.

BUILDINGS

Now, as to buildings. I still cringe when I think of the old
USDA Library. The brown veterans' hospital walls, the long
depressing mental ward corridors covered with Montgomery
Ward linoleum in sickly beige, the Grand Rapids furniture in
golden oak, the dusty venetian blinds—well I could go on and
on. We only need to look around to see the improvement, and
it was Foster who did it. And, of course, we have many fine
new buildings out in the colleges—well-lighted, attractive, well-
designed, *and* air-conditioned.

TECHNICAL SERVICES

The less I use the trite phrase "information explosion" the
better, but some kind of explosion or tidal wave of literature
had started to hit us by the late 1940s, and all libraries were
trying to cope. At the time, there were only a few really large
agricultural libraries of which the NAL was one. Many land-
grant universities had small branch collections for agriculture,
but they often consisted mostly of experiment station bulletins,
trade journals, and a few scientific journals. This partly reflected the more applied nature of agricultural experimentation
of the period before World War II and the background of some
of the older professors who depended more on reprint collections than on libraries. For instance, in 1951 when I arrived at
Davis, then a branch of Berkeley, we had only eighty thousand
volumes in the library. But because of the increase in literature
and the demands of our younger agricultural scientists for more
of the general scientific publications, the Davis library had to be
developed rapidly. Today it houses a collection of about 1.3
million volumes. True, it now serves a general campus, but
probably about 500,000 of these volumes were acquired to support the agricultural program, which reflected the wide diversity
of the agricultural curriculum covering almost all aspects of
human activity. Most of the younger professors in the College
of Agriculture were basically chemists or animal physiologists,
or botanists, rather than applied agriculturalists. As energetic

young scientists, they were producing more literature themselves, thus adding to the flood. Because of the jet plane they had more conferences which generated more papers. Improvements in photographic methods expedited publication and, of course, one had to publish or perish. The same pattern of change also occurred at the other land-grant colleges and was equally evident in government and in industrial laboratories and libraries.

Such rapid growth naturally created problems. We all remember the horrendous backlog of unprocessed material that choked us in the 1950s. Librarians were attacked from all sides because they were slowing up the movement of information. At first, efforts to speed processing largely involved increasing staffs, making full use of Library of Congress (LC) cards and trying to streamline procedures. At NAL, a particular effort was made to improve production of catalog copy through work rationalization and simplification and the use of photography. Unfortunately, these methods were not adequately employed in some academic libraries until years later. Now, in 1977, NAL and many of the land-grant libraries are involved in cooperative projects such as OCLC (Ohio College Library Center) and the MARC (machine-readable cataloging) effort. NAL's data base is computer produced, and the resulting catalogs and index are rapidly generated and widely used. A vast change has occurred in most processing departments, and much duplicated effort around the country has been eliminated. The automation of processing procedures, which was first merely dreamed about, then feared, and finally struggled with, has become an accepted part of the activities of all but the smallest agricultural libraries. Obviously, there has been great improvement in this area.

REFERENCE AND CIRCULATION SERVICES

For the reference librarians in agriculturally oriented libraries, the year 1947 was a bad time. The last issue of the much-valued *Experiment Station Record* covered December 1946, although it was not issued until 1948. There was much weeping and wailing in the land about this. *Biological Abstracts* was only beginning to cover some of the agricultural material. Many of the

great German sources—*handbuchs* and the abstract journals—
heavily used by many scientists trained in the German tradition,
had not resumed publication or were difficult to obtain. Many
textbooks, statistical sources, directories, and other reference
publications needed to be revised. There was no general guide
to agricultural reference works. In 1948, Ralph Shaw suggested
that I compile one. I started work on it but didn't finish it until
ten years later. Fortunately, the valued Commonwealth Agricultural Bureaux (CAB) services continued without a break, and
the *Bibliography of Agriculture*, resulting from the merger of
bibliographic publications issued by Bureau libraries, was
started in 1942. The two great American abstracting services,
Biological Abstracts and *Chemical Abstracts*, began their struggle
to keep up with the literature using subsidies from the U.S.
government. At the beginning of the postwar period, they were
still produced in the traditional way, with abstracts appearing
many months or years after the appearance of the original article
and hand-produced indexes being cumulated years after. Anyone
who was a reference librarian or scientific researcher in those
days will remember with pain the tedious and time-consuming
task of searching in the indexing sources. A fairly complete
retrospective search would literally take weeks. Some scientists,
of course, would have this chore done by a bright young laboratory assistant or a favorite librarian. However, staffs of NAL
and the academic libraries could often not undertake very
lengthy searches unless special funding and staffing were provided. I remember very well several occasions at Davis when we
had to tell a professor that the library staff simply didn't have
time to do an extensive search for him. In other cases, librarians
on the staff would work overtime just to be obliging. Fortunately, useful bibliographies on broadly important current
topics were produced by NAL's Bibliography Division. Nevertheless, retrieving information from the literature in those days
was often difficult and frustrating.

Vannevar Bush recognized the problem at an early stage and
sounded the alarm in his famous *Atlantic Monthly* article, saying "the summation of human experience is being expanded at
a prodigious rate and the means we use for threading through
the consequent maze to the momentarily important item, is

the same as we used in the days of the square rigged ships."[4]
But Bush was a practical man as well as a Cassandra, and,
in the early 1940s, he prepared the principles of an electronic
microfilm searching machine which would expedite information retrieval. A prototype model called the Bush Rapid Selector
was designed and built by Engineering Research Associates of
St. Paul, Minnesota; Ralph Shaw supervised the development
of the model and did most of the bibliographic experimentation.[5] Those of us who worked at NAL in the 1940s remember
the machine very well, since some of us assisted in the experimentation. The machine handled 35 mm microfilm on which
were reproduced documents with associated code patterns of
white and black squares which described the contents of the
documents. One selected the code for the subject of interest,
the machine started the microfilm rolling, and when the photo-
cell recognized the desired code pattern, a copy was made of
the document. Numerous other microfilm searching devices
were developed later, although they were not in wide use because it was difficult to interfile new material and time-consuming to search a complete file for every request. But experimentation with the Rapid Selector did illustrate NAL's early role
in the mechanism of information retrieval. In the late 1950s
and 1960s, as computers were improved in speed and storage
capacity, the abstracting services such as *Chemical Abstracts*
and *Biological Abstracts*, began to mechanize their procedures.
We all know the story—computer-produced indexes, the com-
position and printing of texts with aid of computers, searchable data banks on tape or discs permitting selective dissemination of information (SDI), and on-line services. The story for
Biological Abstracts is well told in W. C. Steere's recent history.[6]
At this time, the NAL staff also started thinking about the computerization of the *Bibliography of Agriculture*, the implemen-
tration of which was completed during John Sherrod's administration.

The impact of these developments on the outlying service
units, including land-grant libraries, has been remarkable. No
longer, except in exceptional cases, are the tedious and lengthy
retrospective manual searches necessary. The busy scientist can

now obtain relevant references quickly through on-line searches, or he can have sent to him, automatically, lists of references on his subject as they appear. In many academic and government libraries today, the automated retrieval services with the proper terminals are part of the reference department and the reference librarians are trained in the use of the terminals, in the development of search strategies for automatic retrieval, as well as in the use of printed sources. Scientists who never came near the library previously are now using these new services. Some have even concluded that the library *is* a useful place after all. And, of course, our old customers are delighted. Their chief complaint now is that journals referred to in the computer searches are in the bindery, stolen, or charged out. At Davis, and I believe at most other land-grant universities, the *Bibliography of Agriculture* tapes have until now proven to be the most useful of the various available data banks for most agricultural scientists. The new CAB tape services are also proving to be increasingly important, and naturally, the *Chemical Abstracts* and *BIOSIS* tapes are widely employed. In any case, the advent of computerization has had a revolutionary and greatly beneficial impact on library reference departments, and NAL played an important role in the great effort.

Another revolutionary development affecting reference and public service as well as processing departments was the improvement of photographic copying techniques. In 1934, at the request of the American Documentation Institute, NAL became the first experimental center for supplying microfilm and photocopies of material on a large scale to scientific workers. Under the ingenious Flemer, head of NAL's photolaboratory, several improvements were developed, such as "continuous fotoprinting" and the "Photoclerk," which helped improve library services and procedures.[7] The big need, of course, was for a faster and cheaper copying process. This process finally was available with the introduction of electrostatic or xerographic methods in the 1960s which have made possible a tremendous improvement in library services and have been particularly useful in agricultural libraries serving busy scientists.

DOCUMENT DELIVERY SERVICES AND
NETWORKS

The circulation charging systems of most libraries in the
1940s were still of the primitive two-card type—workable
for libraries with a small outflow of materials but otherwise
a great bottleneck. Naturally, NAL was one of the first to
use the keysort type of punched cards. However, such cards
were not adequate for the academic libraries with their huge
enrollment increases. Experimentation with the machine-
sorted cards of the IBM (International Business Machines)
type, which were initiated by Ralph Parker at the University
of Texas and the University of Missouri in the 1940s and 1950s,
resulted in a fairly widespread use of this method. Even more improved methods are in use today with the availability of relatively
cheap mini-computers.

For many years, the delivery of agricultural publications in
the United States and some other countries was greatly en-
hanced through interlibrary loan systems. In the United States,
this system involved NAL, the land-grant university libraries,
industrial and laboratory libraries, and, indeed, all research-
oriented libraries. NAL also had quite an extensive system of
field libraries. However, the field libraries had to be largely
abandoned or closed in the early 1950s because of funding
difficulties, although some were continued by the Bureaus.
Shaw tried to fill the gap and provide continued service to
USDA personnel in the field through cooperative arrangements
with land-grant libraries at Nebraska, California, Rhode Island,
Florida, and Oklahoma A&M (Oklahoma Agricultural and
Mechanical Junior College). Although successful, these arrangements had to be terminated because of the paucity of funds.
Plans for a national network were resurrected by Foster Mohr-
hardt as a result of project ABLE (Agriculture Biological
Literature Exploitation),[8] a study conducted by EDUCOM[9]
(Interuniversity Communications Council) which he initiated,
and recommendations of personnel from the land-grant institu-
tions who met in Washington at the invitation of the U.S.
Department of Agriculture. Cooperative services are therefore
again available through contracts with land-grant colleges in

various regions of the country. Cooperative projects involving
on-line service for AGRICOLA (AGRICulture OnLine Access)
and intensive regional collecting of agricultural literature have
also been undertaken in recent years with the outlying libraries.
So, we have in effect a very active agricultural libraries network,
sometimes called ASIN (Agricultural Sciences Information Network).[10, 11] Through my own experience and observations, I
can say that this cooperative effort has been most successful
and beneficial to agricultural research workers in California
and I am sure that my observations will be supported by colleagues in other parts of the country. Fortunately, ASIN may
be officially recognized soon through components of federal
regulations now before the Congress.

International cooperative efforts by librarians have also been
important in improving document delivery and bibliographic
services for agricultural scientists. The staff of the USDA Library
worked with Sigmund von Frauendorfer of the International
Institute of Agriculture, the predecessor of FAO (Food and
Agriculture Organization) and other European librarians to
sponsor an international meeting of agricultural librarians in
1935. For a few years after World War II, librarians were mostly
involved in restoring their services to a normal state and trying
to obtain backfiles of material not available during the debacle.
But in 1955 von Frauendorfer, Foster Mohrhardt, Frank Hirst
of Great Britain, T.P. Loosjes of Holland, and others formed the
International Association of Agricultural Librarians and Documentalists (IAALD) in Brussels. I was also in attendance at that
organizational meeting; in fact, I roomed with Foster and was
delighted to see him elected president. He served in that position
until 1969 and had a most important role in international affairs.
The IAALD has issued a number of useful publications, including directories. Its *Quarterly Bulletin*, first edited by D.H.
Boalch of Oxford and, later, by Govert DeBruyn of the Neth-
erlands, has been a valuable source of information about libraries and bibliographic efforts for agriculture around the world.
It is now issued from NAL with Richard Farley as editor. The
IAALD has also played a significant role in FAO's efforts to
develop the AGRIS (International Information System for
the Agricultural Sciences and Technology) system begun in

1973. AGRIS is now issuing *AGRINDEX* (Agricultural Research Information Index [Department of Agriculture]), a computer-produced index to the world's agricultural literature compiled with input from various national centers such as NAL, international institutions such as CAB and FAO, and regional centers such as IICA (Instituto Interamericano de Ciencias Agricolas) in Costa Rica and the Agricultural Information Bank for Asia (AIBA) in the Philippines. Another international project sponsored by IAALD and FAO is AGLINET (Agricultural Libraries Network). AGLINET's international center is located at FAO's David Lubin Memorial Library in Rome which is directed by K. Harada. Cooperating centers and institutions include NAL, the Library of the Ministry of Agriculture, Fisheries and Food in London, the International Institute of Tropical Agriculture in Ibadan, Nigeria, and the Centro Internacional Tropical in Cali, Colombia. It is hoped that AGLINET will promote efficient and effective delivery of library materials from the haves to the have nots.

SUMMARY

In spite of the great advances, some of them truly revolutionary, which have been noted in this necessarily superficial overview, old problems persist and new ones have arisen. The old work ethic has deteriorated. Staff morale in general is not as good as it used to be. We are all more cynical, more critical, and less hopeful. This is no doubt a general malaise and not confined to libraries. Inflation is a great problem, and many libraries have had to cut back subscriptions, stop buying important new books, and reduce services. This is at a time when the amount of literature continues to increase and when agricultural libraries not only need larger collections in specifically agricultural fields but also must broaden collections into related fields involving the environment, biology, and the social sciences. Because of this increase of relevant literature and also because of automated information retrieval, our clientele is asking for many more items, some of which we cannot always deliver in spite of improved cooperation through networks. We sometimes raise their expectations and then flatly disappoint them.

But in spite of these bleak thoughts, things *are* better. The number of agricultural libraries in the world increased from 944 in 1934 to 2,531 in 1959, according to information provided by von Frauendorfer[12] and D.H. Boalch,[13] and the number is now surely much greater in 1977. In academic libraries, there has been a great increase in library use per student because of changes in instructional methods. Formerly, the professor, who often had a rather parochial attitude toward knowledge, depended entirely on a textbook and a canned lecture. Now the student is often encouraged to read more widely in various souces and to do more independent literature searching. This change, along with greatly accelerated research and a vast increase in literature, has stimulated library development. The library has indeed become a vital instrument for education and research.

In addition, libraries are being operated more effectively through the use of scientific management methods. Productivity per worker may have declined, but in many cases automation has offset this decline. Great improvements in processing techniques and in bibliographic, reference, and document delivery services have occurred through the use of new technology and regional and international cooperation. And for many of these improvements we can thank such dedicated and innovative pioneers as Foster Mohrhardt, whom we are honoring today.

NOTES

1. Frederick W. Taylor, *The Principles of Scientific Management* (New York: Harper, 1919).

2. Ralph R. Shaw, "Scientific Management in the Library," *Wilson Library Bulletin* 21 (January 1947): 349-352, 357.

3. Stephen A. McCarthy, "Administrative Organization and Financial Support of Land Grant College and University Libraries," *College and Research Libraries* 9 (October 1948): 327-331.

4. Vannevar Bush, "As We May Think," *Atlantic Monthly* 176:1 (July 1945): 101-108.

5. Ralph Shaw, "Rapid Selector," *Journal of Documentation* 5 (December 1949): 164-171.

6. William Campbell Steere, *Biological Abstracts/Biosis, the First Fifty Years* (New York: Plenum Press, 1976).

7. Ralph R. Shaw, "Continuous Fotoprinting at the USDA Library," *Library Journal* 70 (September 1945): 738-741.

8. U.S. Department of Agriculture Task Force ABLE, *Agricultural Biological Literature Exploitation: A Systems Study of the National Agricultural Library and Its Users* (Washington, D.C.: U. S. National Agricultural Library, 1965).

9. EDUCOM, *Agricultural Sciences Information Network Development Plan,* EDUCOM Research Report 169 (Boston, 1969).

10. J. Richard Blanchard, *Information Networks for Agriculture,* Chapbook no. 4 (Davis: University of California Library, c1975 by author), Paper delivered at the Workshop on Research Information Networking held at the Agency for International Development, U.S. Department of State, Washington, D.C., on October 24-25, 1974.

11. Foster Mohrhardt and Blanche L. Oliveri, "A National Network of Biological Agricultural Libraries," *College and Research Libraries* 28 (January 1967): 9-16.

12. Sigmund von Frauendorfer, "Agricultural Libraries," *International Review of Agriculture* 31 (August 1940): 255-264.

13. D.H. Boalch, ed., *World Directory of Agricultural Libraries and Documentation Centers* (Harpenden, Herts.: International Association of Agricultural Librarians and Documentalists, 1960).

Research and Innovations in Agricultural Libraries

FOSTER E. MOHRHARDT*

The first major task of the International Association of Agricultural Librarians and Documentalists (IAALD) was to cooperate with agricultural economists in developing an abstract journal for agricultural economics. Sigmund von Frauendorfer, one of the founders of IAALD, was asked to work on the preliminary planning of the journal. In defining the scope of the publication, his initial problem was similar to mine today—identifying and classifying innovation and research. In reporting on his analysis of the agricultural economics field, he stated:

> While in pure and applied biology and in the corresponding farm production branches such as crop production, livestock breeding, horticulture, etc., a distinct line can be drawn fairly easily between studies representing results of original scientific research on the one hand and secondary publications written for extension and popular education on the other, such a clearcut borderline is much more difficult to draw in the economic and social field where opinions, attitudes, and sometimes critical statements regarding controversial questions are so interwoven with results of genuine research and factual information, that it is often difficult to determine whether a book or article should be classed as a scientific study or not. . . .

*Foster Mohrhardt is consultant, Council on Library Resources, and former director, National Agricultural Library.

> A further difficulty typical of a subject belonging to the wide
> field of applied economics is due to the frequent impossibility
> of distinguishing subject matter clearly economic in nature
> from technological problems.[1]

I am certain that von Frauendorfer, as an experienced agricultural librarian, would approve of the extension of this analysis of economics to agricultural librarianship. We have been innovative and successful in solving a wide range of technological problems, but our emphasis on solving day-to-day problems has left little time for carrying out research studies.

In the same manner that Frauendorfer reviewed agricultural economics, I have taken a broad look at the twentieth-century accomplishments in agricultural librarianship. Most of the activities display great practicality and efficiency; many are innovative; but few, if any, could qualify as research. Perhaps this is where the topic assigned to me can be most useful—locating areas in our field for exploration and study. Essentially, then, my paper will provide a general inventory of activities and will be followed by suggestions for broadening our professional work, pointing out fields for exploration.

When I mentioned earlier the paucity of research in the specialized field of agricultural librarianship, I should have pointed out that the broad field of librarianship itself is not noted for its research studies. Emphasis in libraries has been placed upon service, supported by the building and classification of potentially useful collections. Innovations are significant, but research has been neglected.

Essentially, then, we will be identifying innovations. It is often difficult, however, to isolate an innovation and claim it solely as an agricultural library development, since librarianship is a closely knit profession where ideas and innovations are freely and rapidly exchanged—internationally as well as nationally.

THE NATIONAL AGRICULTURAL LIBRARY

Between 1900 and 1910, the U.S. Department of Agriculture (USDA) Library participated in two activities that changed

and improved library and documentation work in succeeding
years. In about 1906, a cooperative system was established
with the Library of Congress for the printing of catalog cards
and their general distribution to libraries in the United States
and other countries.

A second innovation, begun in 1911, was the decision to
provide local and out-of-town users with photographic copies
of articles in the USDA Library. The importance of this service
was recognized by scientists and research workers who coopera-
ted with the Library in setting up the first wide-scale experimental center for providing microfilm and photographic copies
of articles to all scientific workers. Atherton Seidell, National
Institutes of Health, and R.H. Draeger, U.S. Navy Medical
Department, pioneers in microfilm development, used their
personal funds to purchase the camera and film needed to start
the service. Claribel Barnett, the librarian, supplied guidance
and space for the experiment. Copies were provided free to
government workers if the information was needed for their
official work. The American Documentation Institute, Science
Service, Bibliofilm Service, and the Chemical Foundation were
early supporters of this pioneer activity. It is interesting to
note that the American Chemical Society, an enthusiastic early
supporter and a major user of these photocopying services,
later became a major opponent of library photocopying activities. Ralph Shaw, who succeeded Claribel Barnett, pioneered
in the development of the photoclerk and the Bush Rapid
Selector, an early electronic information storage and retrieval
system.

RESOURCE COLLECTION AND SHARING

The spectacular adaptation of computer processes to technical
services tends to overshadow the purposes and resources of
libraries. I am pleased, therefore, to note that the subtitle for
this symposium includes "continuity" as well as "change." The
basic objectives, motivation, and services of our libraries are
characterized by continuity, while change relates to organization, systems, methodology, and techniques.

Agricultural librarians have combined practicality with imagination in building their collections. Their utilization of the process of exchange has been innovative and effective. Research workers, plant explorers, students, and government officials have worked closely with librarians to collect publications unobtainable except through direct contact. The current trend appears to be away from informal exchange contacts and towards formalized international agreements such as those between Japan and the United States, and the USSR and the United States. The U.S.-USSR Agreement on Agricultural Cooperation,[2] signed in 1973, provides for exchange of publications and the study of information retrieval systems.

ACCESS TO INFORMATION

Specialized bibliographic abstracting and indexing services have provided users with effective access to the world's stockpile of agricultural information. A study done in 1969 reported that there were seven hundred abstracting and indexing services containing references to agriculture. Although many agricultural libraries prepare and issue such services, it would be hazardous to single out those that have been or are truly innovative. However, one that can be identified with surety is the *World Agricultural Economics and Rural Sociology Abstracts*, now issued by the Commonwealth Agricultural Bureaux at Oxford, England. Following up on initial studies made by agricultural librarians, IAALD took on the responsibility for developing this journal. Guidance was provided by the International Council of Agricultural Economists, and fiscal support came from the Council on Economic and Social Affairs. This innovative and cooperative effort in the development of an international service opened a door for other activities dealing with agricultural information. The Pesticide Information Center instituted at the National Agricultural Library in 1965 and the Food and Nutrition Information and Educational Materials Center set up there in 1971 are additional examples of innovative services combining the efforts of agricultural librarians and subject specialists.

TECHNOLOGY AND COMPUTERIZATION

Decades ago, the introduction of typewriters in library cataloging departments was questioned and resisted by conservative librarians. There is a marked contrast in the attitude of today's librarians who overanxiously anticipate the latest computerized library adjunct. It would take a hardier explorer than I to brave the jungle of library automation/computerization and declare specific projects as library research or innovation. Manufacturers, consultants, and information specialists have pioneered most of the basic library computer configurations. Ingenuity and innovation have been shown in the economic and practical application of technology to individual libraries. CAIN (CAtaloging-INdexing) and AGRICOLA (AGRICulture OnLine Access) at NAL and similar on-line computerized data bases for search and retrieval of information have extended library services. They are indeed innovative in replacing outdated procedures with more rapid and extensive access to printed resources. I will defer to my co-panelist, John Sherrod, for a judgment on their innovative characteristics in the broad field of library automation.

NETWORKS

More readily acceptable as innovations are the use and extension of these computerized programs in national and international networks. National networks for agricultural information are in operation in many countries. Perhaps the most formalized and comprehensive system is the one supported by the USSR, which combines some measure of coordination of library, indexing, and bibliographic services.

Although the International Information System for the Agricultural Sciences and Technology (AGRIS), which the Food and Agriculture Organization of the United Nations (FAO) approved in 1971, is in some ways similar to the worldwide information systems for chemistry and atomic energy, it is a distinctive development. The first of its two levels of organization provides for current comprehensive bibliographies and for photographic copies of articles listed in the bibliographies. The second phase of the system is AGLINET, the International Agricultural Libraries Network.

Our exploration for evidences of research or innovation has led us inevitably to the critical point of agricultural library service—international cooperation. Probably no other research field or discipline has a longer history of international information exchange than that of agriculture. Librarians in this field, through their international organization (IAALD) and their numerous regional and national societies, have differed from other professional groups in their emphasis on practicality rather than on theory in their programs and projects.

Although traditionally most agricultural research has been supported by governments, private foundations have in the past few decades sponsored and supported specialized research centers. Notable among these has been the Rockefeller Foundation which recognized the need for a specialized library service center as an integral part of the research establishment. Thanks to the imaginative, research-oriented vision of Dorothy Parker, innovative models for specialized research library services have been established. The January 1977 issue of *Agricultural Libraries Information Notes* reports that such centers "are springing up all over the world"[3] but that there are problems in identifying these centers, their publications, and services. Nine located in Mexico, Colombia, Nigeria, India, Kenya, Ethiopia, Peru, and the Philippines were mentioned in the article. Certainly the International Rice Research Institute (IRRI) at Los Banos, Philippines, a joint project of the Rockefeller Foundation, Ford Foundation, and the Philippine government, is a model innovative library information service center. The service extends even to the establishment of a branch office in Tokyo where Japanese publications are translated into English.

My involvement in seven decades of agricultural library activities began and ended with a feeling that there would be much to admire in the practicality, efficiency, and responsiveness of these programs but that there would be few, if any, research accomplishments. As expected, the achievements are numerous and significant, although difficult to assign precisely as the product of a single library. Two major international scientific information conferences have been held in the past thirty years. The first met in 1948 in London, and the second in 1958 in Washington. A study of the proceedings of these meetings supports my feeling that there has been little—if any— significant research in agricultural librarianship.

Hopes for the future are raised by the announcement of a two-year project at the University of Reading entitled "A Review of Information Research in Agriculture." Its purpose is "to consider critically what is already known about the pro- duction, dissemination and use of information in [the field] and to identify specific information problems which merit further study or experimentation." The anticipated date for completion of the study is late 1978.

FIELDS FOR STUDY AND RESEARCH

Even this brief and hurried overview of agricultural library activities suggests the need for research studies in neglected phases of agricultural librarianship. Today, agricultural librar- ians have more opportunities than ever before to carry out experimentation, research, innovation, and special studies. Funds for research, fellowship grants, the urgency of world food problems, scholarly pressures, technological tools, and worldwide recognition of the problems of information and communication provide an encouraging atmosphere for re- search and innovation.

In librarianship as in other professional fields, there has been too much emphasis upon specialized technical development and a neglect of broader relationships and responsibilities. Our host, Richard A. Farley, forcefully expressed this point in answering the question "Where are agricultural librarians today and where are they going tomorrow?" The essence of his reply was: "I keep thinking that we have so much more to offer this food and fiber hungry world, a world incidentally that needs the resources we manage." As an example, he referred to a study made by Richard Chapin showing that agricultural information users make few demands for more resources or services. Commenting, Farley said:

> Should we do anything about this user? Should we stimulate him, hit him with an online search, make him aware of what he is missing or leave him alone?
> ... To me the answer is obvious. Stimulation is the name of our game. But it must be aimed at more than getting him to browse around in our fine books and journals. Above all we need to help him to increase the quality of his research . . . we should respect what he is doing. Too few librarians and information people have personally experienced the research process.[4]

To me, Farley's remarks are more than philosophical observations—they should be taken as admonitions. He would, I hope, agree with my strong feeling that the agricultural library profession must break out into broader fields of responsibility, not only in our direct relationships with users, but also in the broadest scope of our interests—agricultural research, the evaluation and development of primary and secondary publications, all service functions, library tools, and even the promotion of international agricultural development.

To elaborate and clarify these goals, I should submit some specific examples. Librarians are in a position where they are the first to be aware of the gaps or deficiencies of published information—both primary and secondary publications. Few efforts have been made even to survey the scope and availability of information for library users. In 1969, Frauendorfer made a "Survey of Abstracting Services and Current Bibliographical Tools in Agriculture, Forestry, Fisheries, Nutrition, Veterinary Medicine and Related Subjects." This study was updated and expanded by H. Buntrock for the FAO panel on AGRIS and issued in 1970 with the title "Survey of the World Agricultural Documentation Services." Both studies were as their titles indicated—"Surveys." Time limitations made it impossible to carry out detailed studies or reserach into topics such as:

> (a) the extent to which particular fields are covered by secondary publications;

(b) the most practical methods for handling interdisciplinary fields;
(c) biases in services;
(d) unnecessary overlaps in services;
(e) timeliness;
(f) types of output—printed and other;
(g) serious gaps.

Detailed studies could also be made of specific fields. In
1967, Charles Shilling reported on a study in what he termed
"the sociology or world science," which included the inter-
relationships of "the level of economic progress of a nation
and its technology; the dependency of technological progress
and research; and the volume and level of research as reflected
by the types and number of serial publications."[5] Could studies
of this type be carried out to improve our services?

Librarians in Europe and the United States differ widely in
evaluating the importance of dissertations. Most of us have followed the historical acquisition patterns of our countries without making a careful analysis of the significance of such information sources. Could a research study provide better guidelines
for the collection and use of these documents? Similarly, there
has been a divergence of opinion concerning unpublished information. Might it in some areas be worth the effort required
to identify and process what could prove to be a unique source
of data?

I referred earlier to Farley's concern with the librarian-user
relationship. The complexity of information services has made
many users aware of their need for reeducation, guidance, and
initial supervision in setting up informative search patterns. The
challenge of experimentation and studies here includes tact and
diplomacy as well as special tutorial skills.

The broadest and most challenging field for rationalization
and innovation is that of international relations and, more specifically, assistance to developing countries. First, and most important, we need a critical review and evaluation of programs sponsored or supported by governments, private foundations, international organizations, and others. It is my professional judgment that we have too often tried to replicate our systems and

procedures in environments requiring different and simpler operations. Too many librarians in too many developing countries are
meagerly supported, underused, unchallenged, and discouraged.
We have given them excellent technological training, but we have
failed to study or consider social and cultural patterns, rigid
governmental control, and the hierarchical status of librarians
in Third World countries.

Before we respond eagerly to another request from some
international body to assist in enabling some country to have
instant agricultural librarianship, we need to make a healthy
reappraisal of the results of our international efforts. Perhaps
we need more guides such as the *Primer for Agricultural
Libraries* prepared by Dorothy Parker, Frank Hirst, T.P.
Loosjes, and G. Koster or the *Guide for an Agricultural Library
Survey for Developing Countries* by Dorothy Parker and Angelina Carabelli.[6] Such self-help manuals make it possible to
adapt the service to local needs.

My last and largest question is how do we motivate agricultural
librarians to carry out research, innovation, experimentation,
and studies?

NOTES

1. S. von Frauendorfer, "The Story of Abstracting in Agricultural
Economics," *Quarterly Bulletin of the International Association of
Agricultural Librarians and Documentalists* 11 (July 1966): 98.

2. Tatiana Tontarski, "The Library Exchange Project of the US-
USSR Agricultural Agreement," *Agricultural Libraries Information
Notes* 1 (May 1975): 1.

3. Lois Farrell, "Information Centers," *Agricultural Libraries Information Notes* 3 (January 1977): 5-6.

4. Richard Farley, "Director's Column," *Agricultural Libraries Information Notes* 2 (February 1976): 5-6.

5. Charles W. Shilling, "World Information Needs of the Bio-agricul-
tural Scientists," in *Third World Congress of Agricultural Librarians and
Documentalists Proceedings* (Oxford, England: IAALD, 1968), pp. 19-23.

6. Dorothy Parker, Frank C. Hirst, Theodoor P. Loosjes, and Gerrit
Koster, *Primer for Agricultural Libraries* (Oxford, England: IAALD, 1967):
1-72; Dorothy Parker and Angelina Carabelli, *Guide for an Agricultural
Library Survey for Developing Countries* (Metuchen, N.J.: Scarecrow
Press, 1970), 182 pp.

Agricultural Libraries and the Spirit of Cooperation: A Continuing Process

*ANA MARIA PAZ DE ERICKSON**

"Bayanihan—the Philippino word for 'neighborly
cooperation'—makes house moving on the island
of Mactan a laughing matter." Don Moser,
National Geographic 151 (3): 382-383. 1977.

"Inter-Library cooperation is not a new concept for agricultural
librarians in Latin America. You only need to give a glance to
the many bulletins that are constantly coming out of Turrialba,
to learn about the new cooperative efforts of the Inter-American
Association of Agricultural Librarians and Documentalists
(AIBDA) and the Inter-American Program for the Development
of Agricultural Libraries and Documentation of the Inter-American Institute of Agricultural Sciences (IICA-PIDBA)." A lot of
water has flowed under the bridge since Marietta Daniels Shepard made this statement at the Second Inter-American Meeting

*Ana Maria Paz de Erickson is Executive Secretary of the Inter-
American Association of Agricultural Librarians and Documentalists
(AIBDA), Turrialba, Costa Rica; paper prepared with the coopera-
tion of Orlando Arboleda-Sepúlveda, Information Specialist, Inter-
American Centre for Agricultural Documentation and Information
of the Inter-American Institute of Agricultural Sciences (IICA-CIDIA),
San José, Costa Rica.

of Agricultural Librarians and Documentalists in Bogotá, Colombia, in 1968 (19).

This time lapse of nine years has not only meant a continuing process but also a great change in focus of the cooperation and participation of the agricultural libraries and documentation centers in the development of agricultural information as an essential component of agricultural, economic, and social development.

Earlier cooperative efforts among agricultural libraries and documentation centers, at the national level, focused mainly on (1) cataloging; (2) acquisition; (3) compilation of union catalogs of books, serials, and periodical publications; (4) compilation of the National Agricultural Bibliography; and (5) exchange of library materials. Efforts at the inter-American or regional level included (1) the *Agricultural Bibliography of Latin America and the Caribbean*; (2) the *Latin-American Index of Agricultural Theses;* (3) a guide to periodical publications of Latin America; and (4) a bibliography of agricultural bibliographies of Latin America. These projects have been widely reported in the literature, especially in proceedings of conferences, meetings, and round tables in which the subject was discussed (19, 32, 39, 44, 45, 46). Developments of these cooperative efforts up to 1970 were reported to the Fourth World Congress of the International Association of Agricultural Librarians and Documentalists held in Paris in 1970 (32, 39).

This report will give projections of the Latin-American and Caribbean libraries and documentation centers at the national, regional, and international levels during the last quinquennial (1970-1975) and up to the present time.

NEW TRENDS IN AGRICULTURAL INFORMA-TION AND ITS INFLUENCE IN COOPERATIVE ENDEAVORS

The last decade has been characterized as a period of transformation during which major accomplishments have laid the groundwork for national, regional, and international information networks and systems in every field. Agricultural informa-

tion has played a major role, and Latin American and Caribbean
libraries and documentation centers have participated in cooperative endeavors, on a larger or smaller scale. With every pass-
ing day, there is a more urgent need to make a rational utilization of resources for information—human, bibliographic, economic, and technological—to contribute to social and economic
development. Isolation is no longer possible. Libraries and documentation centers, regardless of their size, capabilities, resources,
or location, must share what they have and benefit from the
resources of others. Participation in cooperative endeavors.
whether a library network or an information system, is becoming a matter of "participate or perish." The present reality
demands the promotion and support of the creation of programs
and information services—multinational and interdisciplinary in
nature—with definite purposes and aims.

Cooperative agreements and the mutual utilization of resources, aided by the preparation of bibliographic tools and the
application of new technologies for the storage, retrieval, and
dissemination of information, will lead to better services to
meet the increasing demands for information from research
workers, technicians, development planners, policy-makers,
students, and small farmers. The new trends in information
work have changed the focus of the traditional cooperative
efforts, encouraging every library or documentation center
in a particular area to participate in national, regional, or international programs.

DEVELOPMENT OF AGRICULTURAL INFORMA-
TION IN LATIN AMERICA AND THE CARIBBEAN:
NATIONAL, REGIONAL, AND INTERNATIONAL
COOPERATION PROGRAMS

I. THE IICA-PIDBA

The establishment of the Inter-American Program for the
Development of Agricultural Libraries and Documentation
(IICA-PIDBA) in 1968 by the Inter-American Institute of
Agricultural Sciences, the specialized agency for agriculture

of the Organization of American States (OAS), laid the groundwork for what has now become the Inter-American Information System for the Agricultural Sciences (AGRINTER) (29,
30, 31, 32, 33).

The general purposes of PIDBA were to develop a hemi-
sphere-wide action for the improvement of library and agricultural information services in Latin America, to promote
the better use of human and economic resources of Latin
America and those of foreign aid through coordination and
cooperation in agricultural library programs, and to make possible high-quality research through better information. Other
aims were to provide consultation services and direct technical
assistance for the planning and organization of agricultural
library and information services and to promote a national
agricultural library in each Latin American country, contributing towards the establishment, coordination, and implementation of an agricultural libraries' network.

PIDBA included an intensive program for the training of
agricultural librarians and documentalists at different levels,
as well as a program of publications on library science and
documentation in the field of agriculture, and the promotion
and sponsorship of meetings, conferences, and round tables.
It was also involved in the sponsorship and support of the
AIBDA. As a result of the discussions raised during the First
Round Table of IICA-PIDBA, which was held in Lima, Peru,
in 1967, and from those that followed in Bogotá, Colombia,
in 1968, Rio de Janeiro, Brazil, in 1969, and ultimately in
Turrialba, Costa Rica, in 1972, the basic infrastructure of
AGRINTER was launched (35, 36, 37).

II. AGRINTER

AGRINTER, the Inter-American Information System for
the Agricultural Sciences, of which IICA-CIDIA was designated
as the coordinating center (28), opens the door to the Latin
American and Caribbean countries to participate, at the hemi-
spheric level, in a regional information system, and, as the first
module representing a developing continent, in a worldwide

agricultural information system (AGRIS) and in a worldwide network of agricultural libraries (AGLINET) (1, 15, 16, 17, 22, 27, 28, 31, 33). AGRINTER, conceived as a "network" in its structure, has the following general objectives: (1) to strengthen the planning, organization, and innovation capacities of the countries of the region, assisting them to utilize the relevant information in the decision-making process; and (2) to contribute towards the regional integration of the countries, and the subsequent reciprocal exchange of information and experiences.

The specific objectives of AGRINTER include the following: (1) to contribute towards the creation of the national agricultural information systems of the countries of the region; (2) to assist the countries in planning, coordinating, and operating a regional information system based on a genuine Latin American and Caribbean cooperative endeavor; (3) to support a progressive transformation of the existing information structures in the countries through the application of modern technology for the more efficient storage, processing, and dissemination of the information available in the region; (4) to help make the agricultural information in the country available at the regional and worldwide level and to facilitate the relevant utilization of that information by the different types of users; and (5) to promote better exploitation of existing human, economic, and information resources in Latin America and the Caribbean by strengthening national and regional cooperation, integration, and coordination.

AGRINTER is in full operation at the present time. The basic structure of its system is formed by (a) the AGRINTER coordinating center at IICA-CIDIA and (b) the basic input centers in each country. This "network" structure which centralizes in a "coordinating center" the planning, development, and coordination of the system, with decentralized information input and services, allows for better exploitation of the agricultural documentation in each country and gives more adequate services to users. It also demands a high degree of cooperation from each of the system's components. In the system's initial phase of operation, the components have the following functions:

(a) *Coordinating center:* (1) planning, development, and coordination; (2) financing the organization and coordination of the system; (3) promotion; (4) consultant services, training, and other reinforcement services to the countries; and (5) technical cooperation for the development of national input centers.

(b) *Input centers in the countries:* (1) identification of national documents; (2) selection, acquisition, and storage of documents; (3) recording the information; (4) categorization of documentary units; (5) input of current national agricultural documentation; and (6) information services at the national level.

AGRINTER has the responsibility to adopt and develop adequate procedures to reach its goals and to cooperate at regional and international levels with other information systems. Its first priority is to achieve compatibility with AGRIS, whose methodology it has adopted. The coordinating center of AGRINTER was responsible for determining the adoption of the AGRIS methodology and making the following necessary adaptations: (1) translating into Spanish the system's tools and guidelines; (2) translating the AGRIS Subject Categories; (3) translating and adapting the AGRIS Worksheet for AGRIS and AGRINTER use; (4) compiling a Latin American and Caribbean Core List of Serials; (5) translating and adapting the Council on Scientific and Technical Information (COSATI) Standards for Descriptive Cataloguing; and (6) creating a Data File of Latin American and Caribbean Corporate Authors.

Besides attending to the demands of the national input/output centers, the coordinating center has developed the following complementary system tools: (1) selection criteria for the AGRIS and AGRINTER systems; (2) preparation of guidelines for title enrichment; (3) preparation of classification concordances among the AGRIS categories and the Dewey Decimal and Library of Congress classification schemes; and (4) development of an agricultural vocabulary in Spanish.

The AGRINTER products at the present time include the following:

> —*Agricultural Index of Latin America and
> the Caribbean*
> —Data Bank of Latin American and Caribbean
> agricultural bibliographies
> —Bibliographies of special topics of interest to
> the region
> —Generation of magnetic tapes
> —Development of the Spanish Agricultural
> Vocabulary

In the near future, the services of AGRINTER will be rendered through the AGRINTER SERVICE NETWORK which, at the present time, is being promoted for implementation (27). These services will include:

> —Document reproduction
> —Exchange of specialized bibliographies
> —Exchange of information using microfiche
> as the vehicle for the transfer of informa-
> tion
> —Selective dissemination of information (SDI)
> —Question and answer service, including
> numerical data
> —Translation services and data bank of material
> translated
> —Literature review and abstracting services
> —Agricultural research in progress
> —Directories of institutions and personnel
> —Telecommunication services

The automation era has begun at IICA-CIDIA for agricultural information. With the support of the International Development Research Centre (IDRC) of Canada, IICA-CIDIA started to produce magnetic tapes by computer with documentary data of the Latin American and Caribbean agricultural literature. These magnetic tapes are the input media for the AGRIN-

TER and AGRIS systems and the data bank of agricultural information for automated retrieval. With the first production of the magnetic tapes, the processing of the *Indice Agrícola de América Latina y el Caribe*, the main product of AGRINTER, will be fully automated. The work is being produced both in printed form and on magnetic tape. IICA-CIDIA is now in a position to receive machine-readable input from the countries that produce it.

Other activities of AGRINTER include the implementation of round tables in which representatives of the input centers of each country hold a forum to discuss the system's operation, achievements, problems, and future developments. Since the 1972 round table of IICA-PIDBA, when the system was established, several AGRINTER round tables have taken place: Turrialba, Costa Rica, in 1973 and 1974; Maracay, Venezuela, in 1975; and Brasilia, Brazil, in 1976. The next AGRINTER round table will take place in San José, Costa Rica, in 1978, prior to the Fifth Inter-American Meeting of AIBDA, as a cooperative action from IICA (15, 16, 17, 28).

The training of personnel of the libraries and documentation centers, components of AGRINTER, has been one of the major efforts of IICA-CIDIA. A more detailed description of this activity is given in Part IV of this paper.

One of the most important achievements of AGRINTER is its participation as the first AGRIS Input/Output Center from a developing continent, from the planning and experimental phases to its present operational development (AGRIS Level I). During the earlier planning stages of the AGRIS system, Latin America and the Caribbean were invited to participate in the AGRIS Panel of Experts and in the Implementation Advisory Group.

The decisive policies and mechanisms which contributed to ensure the participation of the Latin American and Caribbean countries in AGRIS were the result of a genuine international cooperative effort among FAO, IICA, IDRC, and NAL. The Latin American and Caribbean participation in AGRIS is at present being extended largely with the sponsorship of an

IDRC technical cooperation package—consultation and financial
support (31).

III. PIADIC

PIADIC, the Agricultural Information Program for the
Central American Isthmus, has been created to respond to the
urgent need as identified by the countries of the region in
three major areas: socioeconomic information for planning and
policy-making; prices, marketing, and production forecasts;
and science and technology. These fields are considered fundamental in the process of decision-making, planning, marketing,
research, and production in the agricultural sciences, particularly
by small farmers, rural families, and other users integrating a
developing society like that of the Central American Isthmus
(25, 26, 41).

PIADIC represents a cooperative effort between the Inter-
American Institute of Agricultural Sciences (IICA), and the
Regional Office for Central American Programs of the U.S.
Agency for International Development (ROCAP). It was created
as a regional program in which all the countries of the Central
American Isthmus participated through their National Coordinating Committees. These committees were constituted by the representatives of the Ministries of Agriculture in each country,
especially from their bureaus of agricultural research, extension
services, marketing, planning, statistics, development, and promotion. Other national, regional, or international organizations
were formed which generate, process, and use agricultural information in the isthmus. PIADIC has a Regional Inter-Institu-
tional Advisory Committee which contributes to the formula-
tion of the program policies.

The basic functions of the generation and management of
agricultural information which the program aims to improve
are as follows: (a) compilation, classification, codification, and
storage of information; (b) processing and analysis of information and preparation of technological information packages;
and (c) transference and promotion of the use of information

through mass communication media. IICA-CIDIA has been a
key institution for the development of the program, contributing its experience and resources in the initial phase of PIADIC.

IV. DEVELOPMENTS AT THE NATIONAL LEVEL

During the last quinquennial, the introduction of the agricultural information systems concept as the major policy of
the Inter-American Institute of Agricultural Sciences for national and regional cooperative development has been instrumental in obtaining an increased sensibility at the level of
national policy decisions, giving information a major role as
a national resource (31, 33).

From a recent analysis made by IICA-CIDIA concerning
the degree of progress achieved by the individual countries
in Latin America and the Caribbean in developing their National
Agricultural Information Systems (SNICA), it is possible to
identify the main tendencies in this direction which, in turn,
reflect the country's degree of global development.

It would take a long time to describe the stage of development of agricultural information systems and services in each
Latin American and Caribbean country. Therefore, some relevant aspects have been selected that can give an idea of the
general situation in the region, such as promotion and coordination; diagnostic studies; national official support; training
activities; and AGRINTER/AGRIS input. The description and
analysis of the situation in each country have already been
presented within the framework of AGRINTER's development
and implementation (15, 16, 17, 20, 21, 24, 34, 42, 43, 47, 48).
Relevant figures on the stage of this development are given in
Table 1.

A. PROMOTION AND COORDINATION

IICA-CIDIA, as the AGRINTER coordinating center, has
systematically carried out promotion activities to involve the
countries of Latin America and the Caribbean in AGRINTER
and AGRIS and to assist the national input centers in improv-

ing their participation in both systems. IICA national offices maintain contacts with the authorities of the agricultural sector in order to seek their support for creating or strengthening the agricultural information system, centers, or services. IICA national offices program meetings, courses, seminars, scholarships, visits to national officials, bibliographic projects, technical cooperation actions, and the like. On the other hand, official missions are carried out by IICA-CIDIA specialists who conduct diagnostic studies, design and formulate projects, assist staff of AGRINTER and AGRIS national liaison centers on aspects of input preparation, plan and participate as professors in courses offered at the national level, and so forth.

B. DIAGNOSTIC STUDIES

Diagnostic studies at the national level have been considered a stong instrument in the planning, development, and implementation of AGRINTER. The spirit of cooperation has been clearly demonstrated in the participation of national and international organizations which have sponsored diagnostic studies, mainly during the last ten years, such as ROCAP/AID, the United Nations, UNESCO, IICA, the Rockefeller Foundation, OAS, National Councils of Scientific and Technical Research, and Ministries of Agriculture. During the last decade, twenty-three countries have participated in the production of diagnostic studies, with the aim of establishing or improving agricultural information and documentation centers and services (2-14, 18, 20, 21, 24, 34, 42, 43, 47, 48, 50).

C. OFFICIAL SUPPORT

It is important to mention the reaction of the authorities in the process of planning and implementation of agricultural information systems. In this regard, eight member countries of AGRINTER have already signed official documents to support their national information systems, and four countries are in the process of doing so. Thus, 50 percent of Latin American and Caribbean countries are participating in AGRINTER/AGRIS.

TABLE 1 Relevant Figures on the Stage of Development of the Participation of the Countries in Agricultural Information Systems and Services

Countries	Promotional activities; official contacts, visits, correspondence, to enlist the countries in AGRINTER and AGRIS	Diagnostic studies	Official support; Decrees, Laws, Agreements, etc., on agricultural information systems and services	Agricultural library & documentation training offered in the countries		22 courses and in-service training offered by IICA-CIDIA	Total number of Trainees	AGRINTER/AGRIS Input sheets sent by the countries to IICA-CIDIA	Input acquired and processed by IICA-CIDIA	Total input processed by CIDIA & the countries Sept. '74-June '77
				No. of courses	No. of participants	No. of participants				
Argentina	x	x	x	3	75	12	87	1.265	—	—
Barbados (1)	x	—	—	—	—	—	—	—	—	—
Bolivia	x	x	x	9	233	16	16	228	—	—
Brazil	x	x	x	4	95	20	253	2.246	—	—
Colombia	x	x	x	—	—	29	124	340	—	—
Costa Rica (1)	x	x	—	—	—	27	27	—	—	—
Cuba (1)	—	—	x	—	—	2	2	—	—	—
Chile	x	x	x	2	45	18	63	1.618	—	—

Ecuador	x	x	(2)	1	15	20	35	351	—	—
El Salvador	x	x	—	—	—	10	10	250	—	—
Guatemala	x	x	—	—	—	15	15	92	—	—
Guyana (1)	x	—	—	—	—	—	—	—	—	—
Haiti	x	x	—	—	—	9	9	103	—	—
Honduras	x	x	—	—	—	19	19	252	—	—
Jamaica	x	—	—	—	—	1	1	25	—	—
Mexico	x	x	(2)	2	18	14	32	171	—	—
Nicaragua	x	x	—	—	—	15	15	125	—	—
Panama	x	x	—	—	—	10	10	8	—	—
Paraguay (1)	x	—	—	1	12	4	16	—	—	—
Peru	x	x	(2)	2	36	28	64	191	—	—
Rep. Dominicana (1)	x	x	(2)	—	—	7	7	—	—	—
Trinidad & Tobago	x	—	—	—	—	1	1	123	—	—
Uruguay	x	x	x	—	—	13	13	60	—	—
Venezuela	x	x	x	3	51	25	76	1.242	—	—
Others (Belize, Philippines, Guadaloupe, Puerto Rico, non-AGRINTER members)	—	—	—	—	—	5	5	—	—	—
				27	580	320	900	8.690	21.921	30.611

D. TRAINING

The concept of training, as considered in this paper and for the purpose of the implementation of the AGRINTER and AGRIS systems, is that of continuing education. This type of training has been a must in the process of getting people and institutions involved in the present concept of systems and networks as opposed to isolation and duplication. The figures of 580 national people trained in their own countries during the last ten years, as well as the 320 people who participated in short courses at the regional level, are considered quite significant within the framework of the national information systems in the field of agriculture. We must not ignore the fact that some other librarians and documentalists have been trained abroad (mainly in the United States and Europe) at the university and graduate level, and in special courses. Even so, it is absolutely necessary to establish aggressive and continued training programs at both national and regional levels.

E. AGRINTER AND AGRIS INPUT

The cooperative effort has been an increasing factor in the process of implementation of the regional system. During the last three years, the total AGRINTER and AGRIS input acquired and processed has reached the total sum of 30,611 items. Some more time is required to make all the countries of Latin America and the Caribbean responsible for their total input. So far just 28 percent of the total input is being provided by the countries, but it is hoped that this percentage will improve in the near future. For the moment, only six countries are contributing no input to the regional and worldwide systems.

Other aspects of cooperation at the national level, such as the elaboration and updating of system tools, union bibliographic projects, and union lists of journals, have been mentioned before. For the near future, there will be sharing of computer facilities, computer programs, and mutual exploita-

tion of AGRINTER, AGRIS, and other agricultural data bases
to offer better services to the information users in each country
and in the region.

THE ROLE OF PROFESSIONAL ASSOCIATIONS IN
AGRICULTURAL INFORMATION COOPERATIVE
ENDEAVORS

Professional library associations have played an important
role in cooperative enterprises. Professional associations have
been instrumental in promoting interlibrary cooperation,
launching cooperative projects, and organizing meetings and
conferences for the purpose of investigating the cooperation
among library associations.

These organizations, created by librarians and documentalists, have achieved unity, and their participation in cooperative
enterprises has opened for them other frontiers in an ever-widen-
ing international field (23, 40).

In Latin America, AIBDA has been a driving force in promoting improved agricultural library services and in encouraging
projects of national and international cooperation. The very
existence of AIBDA exemplifies the spirit of cooperation. Its
development has been characterized by a two-way collaboration
between that association and the organization responsible for
its creation and continued activity—the Inter-American Institute
of Agricultural Sciences, especially its Inter-American Centre
for Agricultural Documentation and Information (IICA-CIDIA),
where AIBDA has its headquarters. Reports of the activities of
these two organizations show that there has been a mutual participation in their projects and that they have worked in close
cooperation to reach their goals for the improvement of agricultural librarianship and information in Latin America and the
Caribbean (30, 32, 33, 39, 40).

AIBDA contributed to what is now one of the products of
AGRINTER—the *Agricultural Bibliography of Latin America
and the Caribbean* (now called the *Indice Agrícola de América
Latina y el Caribe*), which was published by the association for
nine years. During the last two years in which the association

was responsible for its publication, the project became a cooperative enterprise in which the countries that had begun
their participation in AGRINTER contributed to the *Bibliography;* IICA-CIDIA participated in this effort and in financing
the preparation of the indexes by computer. AIBDA has continued to participate in AGRINTER round tables and to promote the countries' participation through its publications
and inter-American meetings.

IICA is always co-sponsor and collaborator in the development of the Inter-American Meetings of Agricultural Librarians
and Documentalists organized and promoted by AIBDA. Both
organizations were responsible for the organization and development of the Fifth World Congress of the International Association of Agricultural Librarians and Documentalists (IAALD),
which took place in Mexico City in 1975. This event provides
a good example of cooperation between library associations.

The library groups at the national level, some of which are
chapters of AIBDA, have also played an important role in the
development of cooperative enterprises in their countries and
have been instrumental in promoting the establishment of
SNICA. These groups have promoted and organized national
meetings and workshops in which the basis for the organization of SNICA was laid. In addition, library groups at the
national level have organized training courses at different
levels and courses on the methodology of AGRINTER and
AGRIS. Especially worthy of mention are the cooperative
efforts by the national associations of agricultural librarians
and documentalists in Brazil, Ecuador, and Peru. These national groups have made a great contribution to the development
of agricultural information in their countries and have demonstrated how rewarding it can be to work together. Group work
by other library associations at the national level was reported
to the Thirty-seventh Session of the International Federation
of Library Associations General Council in 1971 (40).

CONCLUSIONS

No discussion of librarianship is complete without a plea for
cooperation between librarians at the local, regional, and international levels. There are no political boundaries in science—

there should be no political boundaries in the inter-change of scientific information. Every experienced librarian has learned that he or she personally, his or her library, and the library clients as well, have gained more from cooperation than they have contributed (38).

The road to cooperation is not easy, however. Many factors contribute to cooperation—or the lack of it. In many cases, the cooperation is handicapped by the lack of resources: human, economic, bibliographic, technological. In other instances, there is even fear or reluctance to participate in cooperative agreements. There are other barriers—physical, geographic, legal, and administrative—which lessen the cooperative efforts (49). Cooperative endeavors of lasting value require careful planning and consideration, but as long as there is hope and enthusiasm in a few that can communicate it to others, the cause is not lost. As an example, we can refer to what has been stated in this report. In all the accomplishments reported here, there have been many barriers to overcome. In many instances, cooperation has been received from a very few, but the goodwill has always been there.

One of the very first requirements for more successful achievements in cooperative endeavors for developing library and information in every field is a major effort to educate librarians, authorities, and government officials in the philosophy of cooperation.

It is also important to make the national and international organizations sponsoring library and information activities understand the need for channeling their efforts and resources in a cooperative, coordinated, and integrated form—through a unique coordinating agency—in order to avoid duplication of efforts and a bad distribution of resources.

Only when a majority understand the advantages of true and unselfish cooperation will the job of developing national, regional, and international library and information services be—like "house moving on the island of Mactan"—a "laughing matter."

LITERATURE CITED

1. ALVEAR, A., EL AGRINTER, Sistema Interamericano de Información para las Ciencias Agrícolas. Turrialba, Costa

Rica, IICA-CIDIA, 1973. 23 p. (Trabajo presentado al 4o. Congreso Regional de Documentación y 13a. Reunión de la FID/CLA. Bogotá, Octubre 15-19, 1973).

2. ARBOLEDA-SEPULVEDA, O., Acceso a la información agrícola: un programa de acción para México. San José, Costa Rica, IICA-CIDIA, 1976. 96 p.

3. ——, Asesoramiento al Centro Ecuatoriano de Documentación Agrícola; propuesta de programa de trabajo para la puesta en marcha del CEDA. In Asociación Interamericana de Bibliotecarios y Documentalistas Agrícolas. Filial del Ecuador. Jornadas de Trabajo. Quito, 1974. pp. 12-28.

4. ——, Bases para el establecimiento del Subsistema Nacional de Información Agrícola de República Dominicana. San José, Costa Rica, IICA-CIDIA, 1976. 65 p.

5. ——, Elementos para la integración del Proyecto del Subsistema Nacional de Información Agrícola de Honduras. Turrialba, Costa Rica, IICA-CIDIA, 1976. 16 p.

6. ——, Estudio de diagnóstico para el desarrollo de bibliotecas y documentación agrícola en la Zona Andina: Bolivia, Colombia, Ecuador, Perú y Venezuela. Informe de Consulta. Turrialba, Costa Rica, IICA-CIDIA, 1970. 121 p.

7. ——, Los estudios de diagnóstico en el desarrollo de redes de información agrícola en América Latina. In Reunión Interamericana de Bibliotecarios y Documentalistas Agrícolas, 4a. México, Abril, 1975. Informe. Turrialba, Costa Rica, AIBDA, 1977. pp. 67-79.

8. ——, Fortalecimiento de un subsistema nacional de información agrícola (SNIA) en República Dominicana. Santo Domingo, República Dominicana, IICA, Coordinación del Plan de Acción en República Dominicana, 1977. 27 p.

9. ——, Guía para la elaboración de un proyecto para la creacion del Centro Ecuatoriano de Documentación Agrícola (CEDA). Turrialba, Costa Rica, IICA-CIDIA, 1973. 30 p.

10. ——, La información y documentación agrícola en Haití; visión general. Port-au-Prince, Haití, Oficina del IICA en Haití, 1976. 15 p.

11. ——, Inventarios de los recursos nacionales de información y documentación agrícola para su integración en el

AGRINTER. Desarrollo Rural en las Américas 7(3): 286-304. 1975.

12. ——, Trópico americano; situación de los servicios bibliotecarios y de documentación agrícola. Bolivia, Brasil, Colombia, Ecuador, Perú, Venezuela. Turrialba, Costa Rica, IICA-CIDIA, 1972. 41 p. (IICA. Bibliotecología y Documentación no. 21).

13. ——, Una visión general de la documentación e información agrícola en los países de la Zona de las Antillas. San José, Costa Rica, IICA-CIDIA, 1977. 19 p.

14. ——, Visualización del Subsistema Nacional de Información Agrícola en Panamá. San José, Costa Rica, IICA-CIDIA, 1976. 16 p.

15. CACERES-RAMOS, H., Avances del AGRINTER; Informe anual del IICA-CIDIA. San José, Costa Rica, IICA-CIDIA, 1976. 31 p. (Documento presentado en la 8a. Mesa Redonda del AGRINTER, Brasilia, Noviembre 8-11, 1976).

16. ——, Avances del AGRINTER; Informe del Centro Coordinador IICA-CIDIA. Turrialba, Costa Rica, IICA-CIDIA, 1975. 15 p. (Documento presentado en la 7a. Mesa Redonda del AGRINTER, Maracay, Venezuela, Noviembre 24-26, 1975).

17. ——, Informe sobre el desarrollo general del AGRINTER. Turrialba, Costa Rica, IICA-CIDIA, 1974. 9 p. (Documento presentado en la 6a. Mesa Redonda del AGRINTER, Turrialba, Costa Rica, Octubre 28-Noviembre 1, 1974).

18. CARABELLI, A.J., MALUGANI, M.D. y GALEANO, H.M., Creación de un sistema nacional para bibliotecas y documentación agraria para Colombia; informe final. Bogotá, Instituto Colombiano Agropecuario, 1970. 310 p.

19. DANIELS SHEPARD, M., Adquisición cooperativa, con énfasis en los materiales bibliotecarios latinoamericanos para las bibliotecas de los Estados Unidos. *In* Reunión Interamericana de Bibliotecarios y Documentalistas Agrícolas, 2a. Bogotá, Colombia, 1968. Informe. Turrialba, Costa Rica, AIBDA, 1968, pp. IV-B-1-20.

20. ELSO-GALANO, S., Sistema Nacional de Información y Documentación SIDOC/Chile. Santiago, Chile, Instituto Nacional de Investigaciones Agropecuarias, 1977. 10 p.

21. FERNANDEZ, A., Estudio y proyecto de creación del

Sistema Nacional de Información en Ciencias Agropecuarias de la República Argentina. (SNICA-Argentina). Buenos Aires, Universidad, Facultad de Agronomía, 1976. 35 p.

22. GALRAO, M.J., AGRINTER: origen y evolución; bibliografía anotada. Turrialba, Costa Rica, IICA-CIDIA, 1975. 36 p. (IICA. Documentación e Información Agrícola, no. 49).

23. HOLLEY, E.G., The role of professional associations in a network of library activity. Library Trends 24(2): 293-306. 1975.

24. LA INFORMACIÓN agrícola dentro del Sistema Nacional de Información (Colombia), Documentación e Información para el Desarrollo Agrícola 5(1-2):9-10. 1977.

25. INSTITUTO INTERAMERICANO DE CIENCIAS AGRICOLAS—Dirección Regional para la Zona Norte, Estudio de los sistemas de información y datos del sector agropecuario centroamericano. Informe final. Fase I. Estudio No. 5. Guatemala, 1974. 45 p. (Convenio IICA-ZN/ROCAP 73-8 Estudios Agrícolas Regionales del Subsector).

26. ——, Estudio de los sistemas de información y datos agropecuarios en Centroamérica. Informe final de la Fase II del Estudio No. 5. Versión preliminar. Guatemala, IICA-Zona Norte, 1975. 364 p. (Convenio IICA-ZN/ROCAP No. 74-6. Estudios Agrícolas Regionales del Subsector).

27. INTER-AMERICAN CENTER FOR AGRICULTURAL DOCUMENTATION AND INFORMATION, IICA-CIDIA. Proposal for the establishment of the AGRINTER Service Network. Preliminary document for discussion. San José, Costa Rica, 1977. 17 p.

28. INTER-AMERICAN INFORMATION SYSTEM FOR THE AGRICULTURAL SCIENCES—AGRINTER: basis for its establishment, Turrialba, Costa Rica, IICA-CIDIA, 1973. 18 p. (IICA. Agricultural Documentation and Information no. 24).

29. INTER-AMERICAN PROGRAM for the Development of Agricultural Libraries in Latin America—IICA/PIDBA, in Round Table of the Inter-American Program for the Development of Agricultural Libraries, 1st., Lima, 1967. Documents

and Recommendations. Turrialba, IICA, 1968. pp. 11-39.
(IICA. Agricultural Documentation and Information no. 11).
   30. MALUGANI, M.D., Acceso regional a la información
en las ciencias agrícolas: la experiencia de América Latina.
Turrialba, Costa Rica, AIBDA, 1970. 36 p. (AIBDA. Boletín
Técnico no. 8).
   31. ——, AGRINTER, the Latin American and the Caribbean
Information network: a contribution to the AGRIS Level One.
San José, Costa Rica, IICA-CIDIA, 1976. 16 p. Presented at
the Eighth AGRIS Panel of Experts Meeting, Rome, 17-20
May 1976.
   32. ——, I.I.C.A. an instrument for the development of
agricultural information in Latin America. In IAALD World
Congress, 4th. Paris, 1970. Proceedings. Paris, Institut
National de la Recherche Agronomique, 1971. pp. 277-297.
   33. ——, Regional cooperation in agricultural information
in Latin America and the Caribbean. In Workshop/Seminar
on Regional Cooperation in Agricultural Information, College,
Laguna, Philippines, 1975. Proceedings. College, Laguna, AIBA,
1975. pp. 81-96.
   34. MARQUEZ, O. et al., Subsistema Nacional de Información
para las Ciencias Agropecuarias (SININCA); anteproyecto para
su implementación. Maracay, Venezuela, CENIAP, 1974. 19 p.
   35. MESA REDONDA SOBRE EL PROGRAMA INTER-
AMERICANO DE DESARROLLO DE BIBLIOTECAS AGRI-
COLAS, la, Lima, 1967, Documentos y Recomendaciones.
Turrialba, Costa Rica, IICA, 1968. 100 p. (IICA. Bibliotecología
y Documentación, no. 11).
   36. ——, 2a. Bogotá, 1968. Documentos y Recomendaciones.
Bogotá, Centro Interamericano de Desarrollo Rural y Reforma
Agraria, 1968. 205 p. (IICA. Bibliotecología y Documentación,
no. 15).
   37. ——, 3a. Rio de Janeiro, 1969. Documentos y Recomendaciones. Turrialba, Costa Rica, IICA, 1970. 300 p. (IICA. Bibliotecología y Documentación, no. 18).
   38. PARKER, D., Scope of agriculture. In Primer for agricultural libraries. Oxford, IAALD, 1967. pp. 11-18.

39. PAZ DE ERICKSON, A.M., Avances en la adquisición y uso de la información agrícola en América Latina; técnicas modernas y cooperación internacional. *In* IAALD World Congress, 4th. Paris, 1970. Proceedings. Paris, Institut National de la Recherche Agronomique, 1971. pp. 37-65.

40. ——, The role of professional associations in the development of agricultural librarianship and documentation in Latin America. *In* Chaplin, A.H. The organization of the library profession. 2nd ed. München, Verlag Dokumentation, 1976. pp. 94-103.

41. PROGRAMA DE Información Agropecuaria del Istmo Centroamericano, PIADIC. San José, Costa Rica, IICA-CIDIA, 1975. 15 p.

42. PROGRAMME DES NATIONS UNIES POUR LE DEVELOPMENT, Projet du Gouvernement du Brasil. System National D'Information et de Documentation Agricoles. Rome, FAO, 1973. 43 p. (BRA/72/020/B/01/02).

43. RENDON DE PUERTA, N., Coordinación de una red nacional de información (SNI) y un sub-sistema sectorial de información agrícola (SNICA). *In* Reunión Interamericana de Bibliotecarios y Documentalistas Agrícolas, 4a. México, D.F., Abril 1975. Informe. Turrialba, Costa Rica, AIBDA, 1977. pp. 123-131.

44. REUNION INTERAMERICANA DE BIBLIOTECARIOS Y DOCUMENTALISTAS AGRICOLAS, 2a. Bogotá, 1968, Actas y Trabajos Presentados. Bogotá, AIBDA, 1968. pag. var.

45. ——, 3a. Buenos Aires, 1972. Actas y Trabajos Presentados. Buenos Aires, AIBDA, 1972. pag. var.

46. ——, 4a. Mexico, D.F., 1975. Informe. Turrialba, Costa Rica, AIBDA, 1977. 168 p.

47. ROBREDO, J., Centre National de Documentation Agricole (Bresil), assistance préliminaire. Rapport de la première partie de la Mission, 1973. Bresil, 1973. 53 p. (BRA/72029/A/01/12).

48. SISTEMA NACIONAL DE INFORMACAO RURAL. SNIR:

Sistema Nacional de Informação Rural. Brasília, 1976. 58 p.
   49. TREZZA, A., Fear and funding. *In* Networks & cooperation.
Library Journal 99(22):3174-3175. 1974.
   50. VICENTINI, A.L.C., Centro Regional de Documentación
para el Desarrollo Agrícola—CERDAC. Informe final sobre un
proyecto para el establecimiento de un Centro Regional para
la Colección, Análisis y Diseminación de la Información Con-
cerniente al Desarrollo de la Agricultura en América Central.
Turrialba, Costa Rica, IICA, 1970. 166 p.

International Agricultural Librarianship: The Differences

The theme of this symposium, "International Agricultural Librarianship: Continuity and Change," is somewhat confusing. My *Webster's* says that continuity is "a quality or state of being continuous," while change is defined as "any variation or altera- tion." Since the subtleties of being continuous with variations are difficult, this paper will concentrate on the differences in international agricultural librarianship. Differences are stressed, for there may not be one specific role, be it continuous or chang- ing, for agricultural libraries.

During the fall of 1975, I had an opportunity to visit most of the major agricultural libraries of the western United States.[1] During the fall of 1976, I served as a consultant to the agricul- tural libraries in Brazil.[2] In this regard, I perceived the differ- ences between the libraries to be more impressive than the similarities. The libraries visited are not similar in either scope or size. More important, however, are the differences in the role of the libraries as dictated by the development of agricultural research in Brazil and the United States. Recognition of these differences is essential if we are to define a role for agricultural libraries in the exchange of information between agricultural scientists.

*Richard E. Chapin, Director of Libraries, Michigan State University.

The federal-state agricultural research system, as embodied in the U.S. Department of Agriculture (USDA) and the land-grant universities, is unique to the United States. It is only in the United States that agricultural research, extension, and education are concentrated in the state universities, with funding provided by both the state and federal governments. Even the extensive research effort of the USDA is in consort or cooperation with the land-grant universities, not in competition.

The Brazil program for agricultural research is in sharp contrast to the United States program, but it is perhaps more typical of the rest of the world. In Brazil, the agricultural universities are financed and controlled by the Ministry of Education. Agricultural research and the extension service, however, are within the purview of the Ministry of Agriculture. And to make matters more complicated, both research and extension are the responsibility of separate *empresas*, as opposed to being integrated within the Ministry. An *empresa* is, in effect, a government-sponsored business, outside of the control of standard government rules and the bureaucracy and unencumbered by the typical civil service limitations.

Empresa Brasileira de Pesquisa Agropecuária (EMBRAPA) is responsible for the agricultural research in Brazil (see Figure 1). Almost all of the research is done by EMBRAPA personnel at EMBRAPA research stations. In November 1976, there were forty-four EMBRAPA stations: three major centers, twenty-four regional branches, and seventeen product centers. The November date is important because of the rapid and recent growth of the EMBRAPA stations. In addition to the stations, which are fundamental to the research program, EMBRAPA has an affiliation with eight similar state *empresas* and twenty-five universities. In the case of the universities, the relationship is unlike the federal-state program between the U.S. Department of Agriculture and the land-grant universities—university personnel may be involved, but basically on short-term loan to the EMBRAPA stations.

The library and information services of EMBRAPA are provided through the Departmento de Informação e Documentação (DID). There is no one comprehensive agricultural library

FIGURE 1   EMBRAPA Library Network

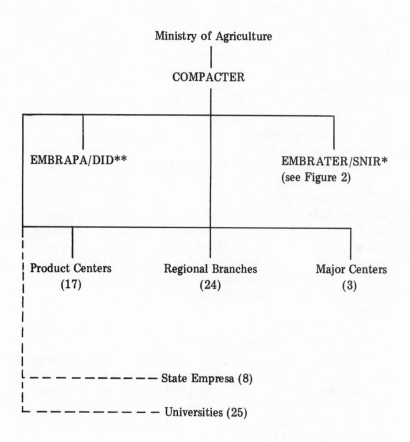

Ministry of Agriculture

COMPACTER

EMBRAPA/DID**

EMBRATER/SNIR*
(see Figure 2)

Product Centers
(17)

Regional Branches
(24)

Major Centers
(3)

State Empresa (8)

Universities (25)

*AGRIS data base
**AGRICOLA data base

at EMBRAPA. DID coordinates collections and services for the research stations rather than maintaining a separate research library. The basic collections are quite small—a core collection of forty periodicals and five thousand books. Theoretically, the growth of the collections is determined by product type or regional specialization. The EMBRAPA libraries resemble information centers rather than traditional libraries. Central retrieval and technical services are provided from Brasilia, using the AGRICOLA (AGRICulture OnLine Access) data base. The research output of the EMBRAPA stations is added to the data base, as are selected publications from selected universities. DID facilitates the interlibrary lending from one station to another. The loan services of EMBRAPA, of course, will be no more extensive than the combined holdings of the station libraries.

Computer-based searches of data and information files are made for station researchers and some faculty of some universities. EMBRAPA intends to extend such services for research and to expand the data bases available. Therefore, bibliographic access is provided, but the physical access, even to Brazilian materials, is limited. If the lack of research at agricultural universities limits the academic programs, so, equally, does the lack of extension work which is the responsibility of yet another *empresa*.

Empresa Brasileira de Assistencia Técnico e Extensão Rural (EMBRATER) is the extension arm of the Ministry of Agriculture. Again, as with EMBRAPA, EMBRATER is part of the Ministry of Agriculture but is technically outside of the federal bureaucracy. Library services of EMBRATER are provided through its Sistema Nacional de Informação Rural (SNIR), which is the counterpart, and perhaps the competitor, of EMBRAPA's DID (see Figure 2).

Although there seems to be little coordination and cooperation between the two *empresas*, the Ministry of Agriculture does have a commission to oversee activities—Comissão Nacional de Pesquisa Agropecuária e da Assistencia Técnica e Extensão Rural (COMPATER). In spite of the commission and a number of laws and directives, there seems to be little coordination of the library services offered by the two *empresas*. For example,

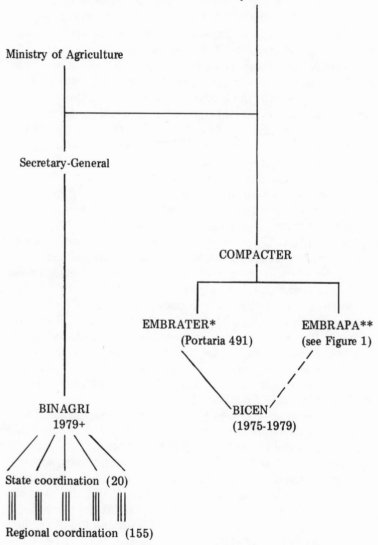

FIGURE 2 EMBRATER Library Network

Ministry of Agriculture

Secretary-General

COMPACTER

EMBRATER*
(Portaria 491)

EMBRAPA**
(see Figure 1)

BICEN
(1975-1979)

BINAGRI
1979+

State coordination (20)

Regional coordination (155)

*AGRIS data base
**AGRICOLA data base

the EMBRAPA library program is based on the AGRICOLA data base, and the EMBRATER services are provided by using the AGRIS (International Information System for the Agricultural Sciences and Technology) data base.

EMBRATER is important to this paper not because of the extension services being provided, but, rather, because it is under contract with the Ministry to develop a national agricultural library for Brazil—Biblioteca Nacional de Agricultura (BINAGRI). Portaria No. 491 of the Ministry of Agriculture contracted with the Ministry and EMBRATER to transform the Biblioteca Central do Ministerio da Agricultura (BICEN) to BINAGRI. The contract runs from 1975 until 1979. EMBRATER was instructed to seek the advice of EMBRAPA, Instituto Brasileiro de Informação Cientifico e Tecnico (IBICT), and other institutions and groups.

The EMBRATER concept is one of a strong national agricultural library center, with emphasis on materials published in Brazil. An attempt has been made, and it will be strengthened, to have all agricultural materials deposited in the central library. Although BICEN has had a troubled past—with a flooded library and the usual problems of consolidating in Brasilia five different libraries from Rio de Janeiro—the collections and services are beginning to take shape. (To emphasize the recency of BICEN, it should be noted that its rather complete holdings are not listed in the only published collective catalog of agricultural periodicals in Brazilian libraries.)

As materials are received at BICEN, the bibliographic information is formulated and processed for inclusion in the AGRIS data base. At the present time, BICEN includes in the data base agriculturally related Brazilian books, reports, theses, and articles from some one hundred periodicals. A copy of the tape is forwarded to FAO (Food and Agriculture Organization of the United Nations) for inclusion in *AGRINDEX*, the printed index. A duplicate tape is maintained as a unique Brazilian file of the bibliography of the agricultural sciences.

A selective dissemination of information programs has been initiated by EMBRATER for the agricultural researcher. Upon request, BICEN will run the researcher's profile against the

Brazilian file. The researcher is thus provided with a monthly list of new information sources from Brazil in the fields of his research interest.

Of particular importance at BICEN is the facility to produce and distribute microfiche. Any of the materials in the library will be copied for scholarly or research work. Also, all reports in selected bibliographies are automatically produced on microfiche. Any library, therefore, may purchase an entire collection on a subject for two or three cruzeiros (25 cents) per title. In addition, upon demand BICEN will copy and produce microfiche of selected issues of periodicals.

The central library, the indexing and bibliographic control of Brazilian publications, selective dissemination of information, and microfiche capabilities make the EMBRATER concept most attractive. It is limited, however, to the 1975 starting date. All of the above, even if more may be desired, are essential for a national system and are now in place. In spite of caveats from EMBRAPA, BINAGRI is likely to develop as the national library. Only two problems seem to remain—the data base and the audience.

The uncertain future of AGRIS and the international library programs of FAO are a cause of concern to the national agricultural library movement in Brazil and other countries. The growing acceptance of AGRICOLA could mean starting over again or, alternatively, a possible difficult merger with EMBRAPA. If AGRIS does fail, and with it a number of national agricultural programs, part of the reason will be the fantastic success and acceptance of the programs from our own National Agricultural Library (NAL).

The other problem—the audience—can be and must be controlled in Brazil. There seem to be three potential audiences for a national agricultural library: the researcher, the faculties of the universities, and the agricultural community. The first of these is being ably served by EMBRAPA. The universities, at least the libraries, have yet to establish affiliations and working arrangements with the fledgling national library. This will surely come, but only if BICEN aggressively develops and promotes new services and programs. The agricultural community might well be served by a national library. If our own NAL is an example, however, the unorganized agricultural community is not an active audience for a national library.

The agricultural universities in Brazil, when compared with the libraries in our land-grant system, would seem to be at a disadvantage without an active, on-going research operation. This is particularly true of graduate programs. If one assumes that graduate education requires a research program, where, in Brazilian universities, are the graduate faculties, the graduate students, the research programs, and research libraries?

The libraries of Brazilian agricultural universities are different in many ways from the libraries of the land-grant universities. The major difference, of course, is in the role of the library. Where the agricultural libraries in the United States are expected to serve the educational, research, and service functions of the colleges of agriculture, the Brazilian libraries serve primarily the undergraduate curricula. If our libraries need large research collections in the biological sciences, the Brazilian libraries need supplementary reading materials for a course that is mostly likely to be based on the lecture/textbook method.

As the roles of the libraries are different, so are the needs and expectations. If American librarians feel unneeded and unloved, they should visit with their counterparts in Brazil. Only recently, for instance, have the Brazilian libraries been supported with separate budgets. The concept of central libraries is so new that there is an informal association of directors of central libraries.

The libraries in the agricultural universities of Brazil will change only as the need for information resources changes. There is some indication that such changes will occur. Agricultural development is one of the priorities of the Brazilian government. As EMBRAPA and other governmental units as well as industry contract with the universities for research, then, and only then, will strong libraries be a necessity.

Let us now return to the theme of this conference—continuity and change in international agricultural librarianship. It would be easy to take a provincial view and state emphatically that unless other countries develop a federal-state agricultural

research system such as ours, with its strong land-grant universities, agricultural research will lag, and with that the libraries
and information systems will be inadequate. Not only would
such a statement be provincial, but also it would be inaccurate!
Exciting and excellent research is being undertaken by agencies
such as EMBRAPA and by the international agricultural research
centers. The following is a quote from the National Research
Council's *World Food and Nutrition Study:*

> Perhaps the largest research contributions to increasing
> world supply of food in recent years have been made by
> the international agricultural research centers, especially
> CIMMYT (International Center for the Improvement of
> Maize and Wheat) and the International Rice Research In-
> stitute in the Philippines. These centers have achieved impor-
> tant research results, such as developing the semi-dwarf varie-
> ties of wheat and rice; and they have become important train-
> ing locations; and they have contributed to the enlargement of
> research capacity in a number of developing countries.

The study continues with statements on the importance and
necessity for basic research to be conducted in the United States
and other high-income countries, and for adaptive and applied
research to be undertaken in developing countries. As is true of
research development, there is no one "best" program for library
development. The emphasis for libraries must be on support of
the research efforts of the home institutions.

Since information services and libraries are required to support research and academic programs, what are the implications
for international agricultural librarianship of the different research styles and emphases from one country to another, of the
goals for food and nutrition research as expressed by the National Research Council, and of the support for developing academic programs in the agricultural sciences? What can and
should be the thrust of an action program resulting from a
conference such as this?

Let me suggest a number of observations that will affect
agricultural librarians at the national and local levels. The first

observation is that the managers and administrators of the agricultural science data bases and, especially, the Foreign Agricultural Office, the Commonwealth Agricultural Bureaux (CAB), and the National Agricultural Library of the United States should reach some sort of accommodation on an orderly merger of efforts. The competing nature of the data bases serves no useful purpose. After observing the input requirements on the agricultural libraries in Brazil—one format for AGRIS and EMBRATER, another format for AGRICOLA and EM-BRAPA, and yet another format for local use—the duplication of effort and the overlap of coverage are obviously counter-productive.

The second observation is that the U.S. Agency for International Development, the World Bank, the United Nations, and other agencies need to be more realistic and develop a better understanding of the total information needs of the countries in which they support library and other information programs.

In Brazil, the aim of the Michigan State University—MEC (Ministry of Education and Culture) project is to develop graduate programs in agriculture. Unfortunately, the libraries have a more urgent need for basic materials and library services in the biological sciences, at both the graduate and under-graduate level, than for resources to support twenty-five to fifty students in a nonresearch-oriented program of agriculture.

Granting agencies, both international and national (including the United States), seem to assume that applied collections, such as agriculture, can exist as separate and distinct entities. In all of the libraries visited, both in the United States and in Brazil, good agricultural collections are built only on good collections in the broader fields of the biological sciences. If funds to support libraries are restricted, either by subject or geographic origin, then the information programs of the receiving institutions will be limited.

My third observation is that there are no outstanding models of cooperative library programs in the field of agriculture. The NAL has initiated and supported some experimental programs, such as service to USDA personnel through the land-grant

libraries and data base searching and microfilming of state agri
cultural research station publications. EMBRAPA has attempted
to develop a network of station libraries, and it has proposed an
extensive microfiche publication program. In neither of the
countries, however, is there a viable agriculture-related program
that has had an impact similar to that of the Regional Medical
Library programs of the National Library of Medicine.

It matters little to say that there are no good models because
agriculture has not received funding equal to that provided
other agencies. That might have been true for the 1960s, but
now we are nearing the end of the 1970s and new priorities
are being assigned to food and nutrition. In Brazil, the increased
production of the agricultural sector is one of the government's
highest goals; the reemphasis on agriculture resulted in the
United Nations' first world food congress; and the president of
the United States, Jimmy Carter, has sought the help of the
National Academy of Sciences "in a major effort to lessen the
grim prospect that future generations of peoples around the
world will be confronted with chronic shortages of food and
with the debilitating effects of malnutrition."[4]

The prospects for food and agriculture research are bullish.
Where are the library programs that would aid and abet this
research effort? What models will be presented for the United
States and for international agricultural information systems?

This discussion brings me to my final two observations: the
need for dynamic leadership in agricultural libraries and the
agricultural scientist's seeming lack of awareness of the advantages of information. If you look at the back of your program,
you will see a world map with all lines leading to the National
Agricultural Library. NAL does have the people, the resources,
and the technology that are required for leadership. The field
is so large, however, that a more likely leadership should be
lodged in a consortium, including, at least the NAL, the CAB,
FAO, and the Instituto Interamericano de Ciencias Agrícolas
(IICA).

The land-grant university libraries are unlikely to play a
leadership role in national or international agricultural developments. They will participate in programs initiated by others,

and they should be expected to play a major role in providing agricultural information services. But the field of agriculture does not loom very large in the eyes of library directors. The unique nature of today's land-grant libraries, serving the entire university, dictates that needs of the agricultural scientist will be viewed and placed in priority along with the needs of medicine, law, engineering, social and behavioral science, humanities, physical sciences, and all of the other academic programs.

Only a few of the land-grant universities have large, adequately supported, separate agriculture libraries; Cornell, Wisconsin, and Nebraska are examples. These libraries and the librarians can and do provide something extra for the agricultural scientists. The norm, however, is not separate libraries, but, rather, service from a central science library or from an overcrowded, understaffed "reading room" (and the quotes are emphasized) that resembles a departmental library as opposed to a complete agriculture library.

If the land-grant libraries are too centralized, the Brazilian libraries are too decentralized. The NAL at least knows with whom to work—the central library administration. EMBRATER, on the other hand, might work with a central library, an agriculture faculty library, a forestry library, and/or an agricultural economics department.

This means, of course, that the U.S. land-grant librarians will not provide leadership because of the large scope of their programs, and the Brazilian librarians will not provide leadership because of the small scope of their programs. Fortunately, there are others, most of you attending this symposium, who can and must assume leadership. But leadership for what? What are the informational needs of the agricultural scientist? It seems to me that the agriculturalists make far too few demands on libraries and information centers.

In the United States, there may be a historical precedent for the lack of library use. Traditionally, in our land-grant concept the problems were identified, research was conducted by the Agricultural Experiment Stations and reported in their bulletins, and word was disseminated by the Cooperative Extension Services throughout the farm community. The system worked and was most effective during the 1920s and 1930s, and even into the 1940s. Then along came "agribusiness." The proprietors of large farms no longer needed the expert advice of the extension agent. Anyway, the best "agents" became "representatives" for chemical firms and implement manufacturers. The traditional experiment station/cooperative extension model passed so quietly that few knew the difference. Our serial librarians knew, however, because rather than the customary research bulletins and technical bulletins, they now received flashy (in four colors) reports of research in progress. The final research is reported in the refereed journals of the societies, not in the traditional publications of the experiment stations.

And with progress came the computers. CRIS (Current Research Information System) was up and running while we were still struggling with project ABLE (Agriculture Biological Literature Exploitation), long before CAIN (CAtaloging-INdexing) AGRICOLA. Even today the research scientists in our colleges of agriculture are familiar with CRIS, but all too few have caught up with AGRICOLA.

While the change in agricultural communication was taking place, our land-grant libraries were doubling in size every ten to twelve years, as opposed to the more traditional libraries which were doubling in sixteen years. This growth took place not because of agriculture but because our agricultural and mechanical colleges were expanding to become total universities. More and more demands were being made by the humanists and the social scientists for current and retrospective materials—materials published when we served only the agricultural and mechanical programs. These new demands meant that the agriculturalist, seemingly satisfied, or at least not objecting vociferously, received a lower priority. With this being the case, perhaps the agricultural scientist was forced to find other ways to meet his information needs.

In summary, if we are to develop new roles for international agricultural librarianship, there must be aggressive leadership which will design new models with an integrated data base to serve the total information needs, not just the applied needs, of the demanding agricultural scientist.

NOTES

1. Richard E. Chapin, unpublished memorandum to Richard A. Farley, entitled "Report on USDA Funded Study to Evaluate the Effectiveness of the 'Memoranda of Understanding' Between Land-Grant Libraries and the National Agricultural Library for the Retention of Agricultural Publications." January 21, 1976. 6 p.

2. Michigan State University, MSU Brazil-MEC Project, *Report #23*, "Library Survey Team Report" (December 20, 1976). 50 p.

3. *World Food and Nutrition Study: The Potential Contributions of Research*, World Food and Nutrition Study Steering Committee of the National Research Council (Washington, D.C.: National Academy of Sciences, 1977), p. 131.

4. Gerald S. Schatz, "Thought for Food: What Must Be Done to Feed the World's People," *News Report* 27 (April 1977): 1, 4.

California Polytechnic State University: Recent Changes in Agricultural Librarianship

*PAULA R. SCOTT**

Before the late 1960s, the Cal Poly Library had a good staff of generalist librarians and a collection of textbooks and supplementary reading to support a basic undergraduate curriculum. Since that time, the library has been changing rapidly in response to a variety of local, national, and international developments. One of the developments is a growing interest in agricultural information, and we, as librarians, are responding to that interest. The major issues revolving around the changes connected with agricultural librarianship at Cal Poly are reviewed in this paper.

In order to evaluate these recent changes, one must know a little about Cal Poly. It is not an ordinary university. The institution opened as a vocational high school in March 1901, and it emphasized agriculture and complementary subjects such as agricultural mechanics.

The library in the early days included a small collection of textbooks and other undergraduate materials to support the curricula of the school. Because the courses were practically oriented, there was little demand for research publications or library staff who were scientifically oriented. Cal Poly began

*Paula R. Scott is reference librarian at California Polytechnic State University.

offering junior college courses in 1927, and, in 1940, the first
bachelor of science degrees were approved. Master of arts degrees
in education were authorized in 1949 and the master of science
degrees in 1967. The school was designated a university in 1972.
From 1933 until 1966, the late Julian A. McPhee was chief ad-
ministrator of the college. He believed in the idea of training
people for agriculture and industry, and the school adopted the
motto "Learn by Doing."

Since that time, Cal Poly has become well known for career
education and currently is experiencing considerable popularity.
Enrollment showed an increase of three thousand students from
1971 to 1975 and then leveled off at approximately fifteen
thousand students.[1] Of those, the School of Agriculture and
Natural Resources has the largest number of students (3,796
in Fall 1976).[2]

SPECIALIZATION OF LIBRARIANS IN SUBJECT FIELDS

In 1968-1969, a number of basic abstracts and indexes were
purchased for the library, including *Chemical Abstracts*, the
Commonwealth Agricultural Bureaux abstracting services, many
library catalogs, and union lists such as the *National Agricultural
Library Catalog*. The index and bibliography areas mushroomed
in size; indexes expanded from a few Wilson indexes on two
counters to hundreds of indexes filling much of the Reference
Room. Bibliographies had to be located in a special Bibliographic Center adjacent to the Reference Room.

The early book selection policy reflected the "lecture and
textbook method which required little use of the library."[3]
In 1968-1969, the library staff made large purchases of scientific research journals, trade publications, and monographs.
Early in 1970, librarians in both the Public Services and Technical Services Departments were given subject assignments in
book selection and collection development. The intent was to
ensure a comprehensive book selection program and to encourage further professional communication between librarians and
the teaching faculty. At that time, the bibliographers in the

Reference Section were generalist librarians who lacked special training in the subjects for which they were responsible.

During the next four years, assignments became more specialized. The library was able to start recruiting librarians with some background in scientific and technical subjects. In 1972, one of the Technical Services librarians was designated bibliographer to coordinate collection development. In 1973, Director L. Harry Strauss hired one librarian with a Ph.D. in biology and another with biomedical library training from the University of California, Los Angeles (UCLA) Biomedical Library, who became the subject specialists for biology and agriculture, respectively. In addition to working on book selection, these librarians devoted time to attending faculty departmental meetings and talking with individual faculty members to promote library use and to encourage faculty participation in the book selection process. In the last couple of years, additional librarians have entered into book selection, so that now almost every professional staff member has certain bibliographical subject areas for which he or she is responsible. Staff members are now expected to read the important journals in their areas of specialization, serve as a liaison to faculty in that department, and search in a wide variety of bibliographical tools for information concerning current and retrospective acquisitions. The large number of people currently involved in agricultural librarianship reflects its growing importance in terms of library activities.

LIBRARY INSTRUCTION

The librarians at Cal Poly have traditionally given tours of the library and special orientation lectures in classes when requested by faculty. Reference librarians have been gradually increasing the number of course-related library tours and lectures over the years.

A library instruction course, Library 101, was prepared in 1970-1971 and taught for the first time in 1971-1972. It is a one-unit course designed to develop students' abilities to use the library as a source of information. The Animal Science Department made Library 101 a required course for the major when the course first appeared and has been requiring students to take it ever since. The number of sections now offered varies from eight to fourteen per academic year, with three librarians doing most of the teaching. Since most of the students in the classes are agriculture majors, the lectures and exercises are oriented toward sources of information in agriculture and related subjects.

The expansion of participation in library instruction parallels the same phenomenon in book selection. Before 1973, basically one person was in charge of library instruction. More librarians began giving tours and class lectures in that year and from then on. This service has been developed to the point that now every librarian working with the public gives in-depth library instruction class presentations in cooperation with the regular teaching faculty. In addition, other library classes are being offered; there are courses in the bibliography of city planning and on information sources in business and economics, and an advanced course on the literature of science, technology, and agriculture. The advanced science course is taught once a year by the science reference librarian.

The change in librarianship from a passive, custodial job to an active, proselytizing profession is most apparent in the new approaches to library instruction. Librarians in educational institutions everywhere are exploring new methods in educating their patrons in special research skills, in agriculture as well as in other fields. For example, there are plans at Cal Poly to make a slide-tape presentation for ornamental horticulture classes using slides of plants and the associated reference tools. Librarians are writing information sheets explaining the use of basic bibliographic tools in the fields of animal science, crop science, and natural resources management. Two librarians have produced a sixty-four page handbook for the Cal Poly Library entitled *Guide to the Literature of Biology and Agriculture*, which is used as a textbook for the advanced science library class and is currently being revised and enlarged.

It is apparent to the librarians working in biology and agriculture at Cal Poly that students are seeking to develop the skill of finding information and are not satisfied with acquiring information from class lectures. The philosophy of limiting education to classroom lectures and laboratories is obsolete. Librarians are instrumental in giving these students the tools to develop research abilities in the library.

INTERLIBRARY LOANS

Ten years ago, an interlibrary loan was considered a "special" item strictly for faculty and graduate students. Now many undergraduate students consider the loans standard procedure in any major research project. The increased costs of periodicals with subsequent cancellations and the new possibilities for obtaining materials from other libraries have completely changed the concept of interlibrary loan services. Cal Poly Library Director Norman Alexander foresees that in the near future the interlibrary loan operation will be as large as or larger than the existing reference services.

From compiled statistics, it can be concluded that interlibrary loans will be an important factor in agricultural librarianship in the future. The number of requests for agricultural materials, while not large, indicates that there may be an increasing awareness of Cal Poly as a source of agricultural publications. The overall increases reflect the development of a local network, TIE (Total Interlibrary Exchange), and the broadening of contacts and cooperative efforts in many libraries. The agricultural faculty and students are requesting more interlibrary loans, a fact which reflects their growing interest in library-oriented research. The data base access will expand the information retrieval capability on all subjects and connect Cal Poly directly with the major information services, including the National Agricultural Library's AGRICOLA (AGRICulture OnLine Access).

COMMENTS AND CONCLUSIONS

According to Ariès, the years since 1970 have been particularly significant for agricultural librarianship throughout the world. He notes the following four changes in the field during the period 1970-1975: (1) an increased political influence connected with automated information services; (2) the entry of the developing countries into the group of information-producing countries; (3) international cooperation on a greatly increased scale; and (4) the entry of new types of people into the profession.[4]

It has been observed that the Cal Poly Library has also been changing since 1970, which no doubt reflects the broader changes noted by Ariès. The California Polytechnic State University is known for its occupationally centered curricula; it offers instruction in practical skills which more and more students are anxious to acquire. Combined with Cal Poly's success is the increased importance of the library.

Librarians are making themselves more important by becoming more active in the educational process at Cal Poly. They are participating in instruction, with the responsibilities of regular faculty members—teaching classes, organizing workshops, and presenting special seminars.

Cal Poly librarians are attempting to become "information specialists" by developing expertise in subject areas. In particular, the reference librarian positions associated with biology and agriculture at Cal Poly are moving away from general reference work somewhat and toward more subject-specific teaching and research activities. New people being hired in librarianship are usually required to have a subject specialty, and this is the case at Cal Poly. The new reference head position advertisement recommends a Ph.D. in the sciences, in addition to the standard M.L.S. and supervisory experience. As a result of this specialization, librarians can offer more in-depth service to their clientele.

The staff at Cal Poly are increasing contacts with other institutions by expanding interlibrary loan services and tapping the automated information systems. There are also more professional contacts at professional meetings. Librarians see professional library organizations as an important part of their working lives. All of these trends seem to be pointing toward a broader and more international outlook for librarians.

The literature in agriculture is scattered, appearing in government documents, trade publications, and scientific research materials. Brennan outlines a tri-level flow of information in these major types of literature.[5] Because the information is dispersed so widely and so many documents are produced each year (two hundred thousand), bibliographic control of agriculture is still unequal to that in chemistry, physics, and medicine.[6] Agriculture is becoming more dependent on scientific knowledge as physics, chemistry, and molecular biology play a larger role in agricultural research. As agriculture becomes more interdisciplinary, the agricultural library will assume more features of a life science library covering broad areas of the biological and life sciences.[7]

Increased demands for agricultural information services are likely to occur in the future, along with larger populations and a more complex agricultural technology. There is a definite need, then, for agricultural librarians to recognize the new requirements of the agricultural community as well as the basic changes in librarianship, and to create the new centers of agricultural information of the future. Effective networks, automation, and professional organizations working together on an international scale may begin to meet this need. Hopefully, we as agricultural librarians can unite in our perceptions of ourselves and bring about solutions to the problems of the future.

NOTES

1. L.H. Dunigan, *Report on Enrollment Trends and Student Characteristics* (San Luis Obispo, Calif.: California Polytechnic State University, 1975).

2. California Polytechnic State University, San Luis Obispo, *Announcements, 1977-79 Catalog Issue* (San Luis Obispo, Calif., 1977), pp. 36-37.

3. J. Richard Blanchard, "The History of Agricultural Libraries in the United States," in *Agricultural Literature: Proud Heritage— Future Promise* (Washington, D.C.: Associates of the National Agricultural Library, Inc. and the Graduate School Press, U.S. Department of Agriculture, 1977), p. 230.

4. Ph. Ariès, "Evolution of Agricultural Information Services in the

World: General Trends and the Present Situation," *International Association of Agricultural Librarians and Documentalists, Quarterly Bulletin* 20, 3/4 (1975): 105-110.

5. P.W. Brennan, "Informational Flow in American Agricultural Literature," *International Association of Agricultural Librarians and Documentalists, Quarterly Bulletin* 20, 2 (1975): 86-93.

6. Hermes D. Kreilkamp, "The National Agricultural Library's Data Base: AGRICOLA," *College and Research Libraries* 38 (July 1977): 298-303.

7. Brennan, op. cit., pp. 86, 91.

International
Archival Cooperation—
A Catalyst for Development

*JAMES B. RHOADS**

I have just returned from two meetings in Europe that centered on critical issues of international archival cooperation. The National Archives of the United States and other archives throughout the world have in the last thirty years embarked on many international projects for the archival profession, and those projects increasingly are involved in diplomatic and political questions. What I find amusing is that though those political problems can be serious and difficult to resolve, the small matters of logistics and social events often are more important.

One incident involves the first Russian scholarly delegation to come to the United States after Stalin's rule in 1958. They were to meet at Indiana University, but their hosts had not received a word from them or the Soviet Embassy. They arrived on a football Saturday having spent their entire stipend on a taxi ride from Chicago to Bloomington, Illinois. Some kind soul got them from Bloomington, Illinois, to Bloomington, Indiana, but they had to stay in private homes until the football crowd left that weekend.

*James B. Rhoads is Archivist of the United States, National Archives and Records Service, U.S. General Services Administration, Washington, D.C.

That may be lesson number one in international cooperation. You have to get together first, and then the work can
begin.

The second lesson may be that the social events are important for the forms and friendships, not the substance. Russian
archivists have learned that to be toasted with water is not an
insult, once they learned Americans can put their hearts, if
not their heads, into many toasts. And last year when I succeeded
F.I. Dolgikh, the director general of the Soviet archives, as
president of the International Council on Archives, I knew he
would want us to embrace on the podium. Dolgikh is a fine
son of Mother Russia, but he is only five and a half feet tall.
We embraced.

The National Archives has worked with the Soviet archivists
in a number of international organizations and on a number of
projects, and I think those efforts illustrate the success and
problems of cooperation in international cultural affairs. The
Soviet archivists belong to a far different tradition than do
American or Western European archivists. Until 1960, the
Main Archives Administration was part of the Soviet state
security organization, the KGB. Scholarly access to archival
materials and state secrecy have far different meanings in our
two countries. Nonetheless, archivists from the Soviet Union
and the United States have learned each other's theories and
practices, have worked together in committees of international
organizations, and are now working on a joint documentary
publication project.

No one would say that the negotiations and work have been
easy, nor will archival cooperation between the two nations
shake up the SALT talks. But there has been progress, and archivists in the two countries now know each other. The archives of
the two countries have certainly benefited from the experiences.
This is what we ask of our international projects—do they improve the institutions involved in the project, and do they increase understanding between archivists? The priorities are in
that order, but both factors are essential to continue international archival cooperation and exchange.

May I say at this time how pleased I am to speak at this symposium in honor of Foster Mohrhardt, for he was one of the first to see and support the international archival community as an important element in the information universe of libraries, archives, and documentation. In his role at the Council on Library Resources (CLR), his interest in archives—I want to use the word "fostered"—encouraged CLR to assist the International Council on Archives (ICA) and the ICA's Committee on Archival Development (which is specifically responsible for aid and assistance to Third World archival institutions and archivists). That support, which is primarily for expanded staff, has been of great help to ICA as its worldwide responsibilities increased. Foster, beyond having fine qualities as an individual and as a friend, certainly promoted the expansion and value of international archival cooperation. My thanks to him and to the National Agricultural Library for giving me the opportunity to express my profession's gratitude to him publicly.

The development of international archival cooperation on a continuing basis began after World War II. Several international meetings had taken place before the war, but as part of the International Council on Historical Sciences or the International Federation of Library Associations. Against the background of wartime destruction and transfer of many archives, Solon J. Buck, then Archivist of the United States, called for the protection of records during wartime and the establishment of an international organization to deal with the common interests of archivists throughout the world.

His presidential address to the Society of American Archivists in 1946, entitled "The Archivist's 'One World,'" suggests the optimism of the early postwar period, but his insistence on the uniqueness of archival materials in every country, and the necessity of preserving that worldwide archival heritage, remains the basis of international archival cooperation today.

American archivists who attended the first ICA congresses in Europe were new to such international meetings, but their published reports were full of excitement. They had learned of archival work in medieval languages and seals, which we do not have to handle. They also pressed the American concepts of records management, microphotography, and greater access to archives. The excitement and issues remain today, slightly altered given the changes and progress made, but they remain a major part of the international activities of the archival profession.

UNESCO helped sponsor the first congress in Paris in 1950, and Paris has remained the center of ICA business. Until the last decade, ICA had an essentially European character. Most of its work involved the exchange of information at congresses, a yearly round table, and a number of publications. A journal, *Archivum*, was published along with international guides to archives on particular topics and an international glossary of archival terminology. These were the first priorities of a young profession at the international level, and the International Council on Archives has accomplished much in the thirty years since its creation.

In the 1960s, North American and Eastern European archivists became more involved in ICA, and more recently, archivists from the developing nations have become a major force in the international archival community. They have attended ICA congresses and round tables, and have worked in the committees of ICA. At the 1976 congress, the constitution was amended, requiring that one of the two vice-presidents be from a Third World country.

With the financial assistance of UNESCO and other organizations, archivists trained in the specific fields of preservation, microfilming, and archival architecture and equipment were sent to many countries as consultants for periods from two weeks to six months. These consultants often worked on specific operational problems or trained archivists in the developing countries as they were establishing national archival institutions. It was hoped that those who received the training would, in turn, train others in their own countries or regions.

Those early exchanges were often between metropolitan powers and former colonies, but later regional training centers in the Third World were seen as politically and professionally necessary. Often the geographical areas presented unique preservation problems, and the nascent programs were usually far different from the long-established archives of Western Europe or the huge holdings of the National Archives here in Washington.

The idea of regional archival training centers in the Third World was supported by ICA, UNESCO, and the United Nations Development Fund. Now there are centers in Ghana, Senegal, and Argentina, with plans for centers for Southeast Asia and possibly in the Arab world. These centers are able to teach archival theory and practice to a much larger group of people, at less cost, and with a much greater emphasis on the specific archival needs of emerging nations. The centers in Dakar, Accra, and Cordoba are within the library schools at the universities in those cities. Establishment of the centers was not easy, but we see them as perhaps the most important contribution to developing archival programs throughout the Third World.

International cooperation achieves its greatest success in such training work. Archival theory and practice can be disseminated throughout the world, modified to local conditions, and used to build archival collections and institutions. The development programs of ICA, UNESCO, the United Nations Development Fund, and the International Archival Development Fund are catalytic; they encourage, they teach, and they support burgeoning programs that can use the assistance provided. We think the training of personnel is the most catalytic aid we can offer.

Other entities have sent materials or monies to equip preservation or reproduction shops in archives or to prepare certain studies and manuals. In all the assistance programs, one criterion for the aid has been the initiative of the receiving nation or archives. We think it is necessary for there to be a willingness, even an eagerness, to use the aid and to go beyond the limits that the usually small contributions can make. And we earnestly rejoice that archives in the developing countries, whose staffs are often too small and poorly paid, are attempting to preserve records in totally inadequate facilities. They use the assistance provided them and build upon it, making their institutions

viable and gaining recognition from their governments and other
users.

Another point we have emphasized in our work with the archives of developing countries is the economic and social utility
of archival sources. Few developing nations have the funds to
support much historical study, although national identity
through its historical sources can be significant to an emerging
nation. But archives, like libraries, can be great resources for
economic development. Records of the past give administrators,
economists, and scientists a view of what has been done, allow
them to build on the experience of previous work, and can save
large amounts of money.

We see these economic and administrative uses of archives as
of particular value to agricultural economies. Land records,
maps, crop reports, meteorological records, and export and im-
port data of farm products and supplies are only some of the
types of archives that can be of great importance to the present
economies of the developing nations. Records may also reveal
past land usage, drought patterns, trade routes, consumption
rates, and other facets of past agricultural economies.

I must say that though we see our archives as great sources
of information for agricultural economists and scientists, such
records are not overused by those groups. We see a presentism
in both fields that often blinds them from even thinking of the
past. While this emphasis is unfortunate, we are seeing more
scientists and social scientists using archival sources.

You may have read of the scientists who went back to the
American and German World War II records on synthetic rub-
ber experiments to learn what was done in another time of
energy shortage. The Brookings people are doing a major study
of energy policies and are now looking at records in our presidential libraries and at the National Archives to see how such
policies were, in fact, developed in the past. Last year we sponsored a conference on agricultural history, and we were pleasant-
ly surprised at the number of nonhistorians who attended.
Agricultural economists, businessmen, and farmers came to find
out what had happened in American agriculture. Some obviously came from simple intellectual curiosity, but others saw

the conference sessions linked to their own present work. I dare say some of you are here today for the same reason.

We encourage our Third World colleagues to attract similar researchers to their archives. Most are in countries where the predominant industry is agriculture, and where the experiment stations and agricultural library systems are often just beginning. I believe that, in time, archives will become a fundamental part of the agricultural information services in those countries.

Such use, however, has created a vexing political question in the international archival world. Many of those archives are still in the capitals of the former colonial powers. Most of the records created in the colonies were kept in the new nations when independence came, but the colonial records in the capital of the home governments are also essential and are wanted by the new nations.

The International Round Table on Archives just concluded in Italy discussed the issue of records that are located in one country but have great value to another country. War and colonization created the problem, and though there have been some exchanges of documents, mass transfers of original records do not seem likely. UNESCO helped sponsor the Round Table, and we hope that it and other organizations will be able to fund microfilming projects that will allow two or more nations to have the information from records kept in one.

The United States filmed German and Japanese records after World War II and returned the originals to those countries, and the Dutch are filming records from their colonial experience in Indonesia for that country. But, of course, the British and French have the biggest responsibilities in this area of potential international archival cooperation.

I have welcomed the opportunity to review the history and hopes of our international work. Such cooperation will enrich the informational resources of all nations. Although, at times, such international efforts may seem small and difficult to maintain, our labors to increase the information resources throughout the world are critical to the world communities of archivists, librarians, researchers, and consumers—all of us.

The Future of
International Cooperation
in Agricultural Information

JOHN SHERROD*

The most valued book in my private library is one coedited and autographed by Foster Mohrhardt. He has given me many books over the years dealing with an agricultural topic dear to both of us. For these gifts, and for our long professional association, I am grateful. For our personal friendship, I am deeply honored. And so, on this special occasion of tribute to Foster, I particularly am pleased to be here in this great library which could have been built only through his untiring and devoted efforts.

As for the topic of my presentation, I have decided to exercise an author's prerogative and to change the title from that announced in the original program. The change is not a significant one, but I do want to consider the future of international cooperation, as I see it, in agricultural information. International cooperation in the collecting, processing, and sharing of scientific and technical information takes many forms and can be accomplished through many different agencies. In my view, however, programs can be considered truly international in character only if their conduct is channeled through an international organization. Bilateral agreements between governments or government agencies, or internationally oriented programs of

*John Sherrod is library and information consultant, Rockville, Maryland.

national organizations do not qualify under this definition.

In addition to this perhaps narrow definition, I would like to add an assumption with which I am sure this audience will agree. Scientific and technical progress is the major resource for development of the modern world. The future of each nation as well as that of all mankind is based now more than ever before on knowledge rather than on any material resource. Therefore, success or failure on the national or international level depends significantly on the spread and exchange of useful, scientific, and technical information.

GLOBAL CRISIS

Many of the crises affecting local societies are direct consequences of events occurring around the world. John McHale describes this phenomenon as follows:

> In terms of an information environment, our world has shrunk swiftly, in just over two generations, from one whose surface was still incompletely known and whose peoples were fairly remote strangers to one another, to one which is a continuous neighbourhood, in which, theoretically, no person is more than a few hours distant from all others and in which communications may be practically instantaneous. Man-made satellites encircle this neighbourhood many times in one day, and the repercussions of decisive events affecting any part of the human family are swiftly felt around the globe.[1]

Ervin Laszlo sees the situation so:

> And for now, the rich nations continue to get richer and the poor to get poorer. Disparity in wealth between nations now exceeds the fantastic ratio of 40:1; and half of the world's population exists at or below the poverty line. Millions die every year of malnutrition. Similar inequalities obtain in other areas measured by economic indicators: energy consumption, food production, usage of raw materials, pollution generation, population growth and per capita income.[2]

The new technical developments which have created so
many tensions and crises also have forced mankind to interact more strongly, whether we like it or not. If we survive
these problems for the next few years, we clearly are headed
toward a global civilization. Only parochial minds could imagine
otherwise.

PREDICTING THE FUTURE

We cannot see into the future and predict with certainty what
the nature of the new world order will be like. It may even be
futile to do so. However, what lies ahead is important to you
and to me. We may not like what we see, but, if seen in time,
we may be able to take more appropriate action. Here, of
course, I am not making moral judgments nor am I discussing
what should or could happen. I am describing what I believe is
likely to happen based on my own experiences and those of
writers with whom I agree.

Scientific methods of looking ahead generally lie along two
lines. In one, we produce mathematical extrapolations of historical trends. In the other, a technique known as Delphi is
used in which the collective judgments of the best available
minds are used to identify and estimate the impact of the most
critical or significant factors affecting any given outcome.

I have chosen neither of these approaches for what should be
obvious reasons. Instead, I have decided to examine, by intu-
itive assessment and review of the literature, the political, social,
economic, and technical factors which I believe will have decisive effects on the future of international cooperation in agricultural information.

POLITICAL FACTORS

The international exchange of scientific and technical information has been recognized, in theory at least, by governmental
and private institutions around the world. This process stems
from the traditional cooperation among both scientists and

librarians. In a way, then, it could be said that national policies generally favor efforts that promote these information programs.

Unfortunately, the United States has no comprehensive national information plan. The consequences of this lack can range from humorous to tragic, depending on one's point of view. Take, for example, the case of the role of the United States in the development of the International Information Systems for Agricultural Sciences and Technology (AGRIS).

In 1968 in Bogotá, in a paper[3] presented at the Second Meeting of the Inter-American Association of Agricultural Librarians and Documentalists (AIBDA), and while director of the National Agricultural Library (NAL), I first proposed establishment of the system which later became known as AGRIS. I supported AGRIS vigorously while at NAL, in line with what I perceived as at least a de facto policy favoring international cooperation in information. By 1977, however, the U.S. policy toward AGRIS seemed to undergo a dramatic shift. The new director of NAL, with different perceptions of program priorities, stated in congressional hearings that "plans for the U.S. withdrawal from the system are now being made."[4]

How is it possible that a government agency could take the lead in establishing an international information system and then unilaterally propose action that in effect would kill the system before an adequate evaluation of its service was made? It could only happen in the absence of any meaningful policy and where agency policy-makers in general have little or no interest in the operation of science information programs. This is true not only in agriculture, of course, but also in many other federal agencies where the information program directors are free to negotiate individual programs of international cooperation as they see fit. The absence of any national goals or planning in this area totally confounds our foreign friends, and understandably so.

Unfortunately, I see no early way out of this dilemma. Bill Knox described it so clearly in a recent paper he presented at the American Society for Information Science meeting in Chicago.[5] There is no public perception of an information problem; consequently, there will be no national information policy except for bits and pieces for a long time.

There is a second and growing area of concern to me with respect to the political aspects of international cooperation in agricultural information. The so-called Third World countries have gained political strength in the United Nations and its specialized agencies. They have been insisting, with growing fervor, that their specialized needs be met through increased information resources. They fully believe, rightly or wrongly, that a higher level of economic independence can be achieved through transfer of technical information. For the advanced nations, such as the United States, to accede to these demands could mean some temporary reductions in overall system efficiency. Understandably, the advanced nations with extensive vested interests in their national information programs are reluctant to do so. Thus we have another dilemma.

Inevitably, the trend will be toward more politicalization of our information services. Where the information service involved is government service, such as with agriculture in the United States, the politician may have the last word. Where the government's role is a minor one, such as with agricultural information in the United Kingdom, cooperation at the international level cannot be obtained by government fiat.

On the whole, I am not encouraged by the amount of progress to date toward any significant policy definitions in information at the national level. The United States clearly is the major power in the world when it comes to information, as with so many other things. And, as in some other areas, its leadership here has been less than inspiring.

SOCIAL FACTORS

The real impact of information systems in agriculture, or in nearly any other subject area, is unknown. Raymond Aubrac,[6] who attended the Bogotá meeting referred to earlier and who was instrumental in bringing AGRIS to an operating level, discusses in a recent article the problems of obtaining practical

results at the farmer's level from any of our so-called sophisticated information systems. In what might be considered a
modest understatement, he notes, "There is undoubtedly a
considerable stock of knowledge being inadequately used."

There have been few user studies of note, but a recent report[7] by the Office of Telecommunications provides fantastic
insights into the generation and use of information in each of
the major industries within the United States. This study found
that, as early as 1967, total information activity accounted for
nearly half of our total GNP. Approximately 21 percent of
GNP originated in the secondary information sector (information produced for internal consumption only). Surprisingly,
agriculture had the lowest percentage (1.7 percent) of any industry. The free information provided through public subsidy
by the Department of Agriculture accounts for some of this,
but the low figure may also suggest that there is little latent or
potential market for new agricultural information programs.

Other studies have shown equally disappointing results with
respect to society's response in general to scientific and technical
information services. Alex Tomberg reported at the 1977 Cran-
field Conference[8] that growth in the use of on-line bibliographic
services has recently declined in both the United States and in
Europe. There is growing evidence that the majority of on-line
users do not find the results sufficiently valuable to use the
service a second time. And the general unwillingness of users
to pay for information services has been documented repeatedly.

In spite of many millions of dollars expended by federal
agencies in operating scientific and technical information systems, there remains little recognition or understanding of their
purpose or utility at either the levels of the policy-maker or
the general user. It seems unlikely that this poor image will
improve appreciably in the next few years.

ECONOMIC FACTORS

Closely related to social factors are those economic considera-
tions which may ultimately determine the success or failure
of an information system. As costs of services go up, use tends

to go down. As use goes down to a certain level, we lose some of the economies of scale. In late 1976, the National Science Foundation released the first comprehensive summary and analysis of data on the production and use of scientific and technical information in the United States.[9] This report indicates that the cost of scientific and technical communication is growing faster than the GNP. The growth of these expenditures is particularly pronounced when compared to research and development funding levels. If the trend continues, funds for information will compete more heavily with research funds, and this pressure may become critical for information programs.

A recent report by Forecasting International projects an exponential increase in the cost per year of information dissemination within the scientific and technical community between 1970 and 1990, reaching a level of almost 10 dollars per year.[10] Communication costs soar when crossing national boundaries. For example, according to a report by the International Institute for Applied Systems Analysis[11] in Vienna, the cost of an international circuit may be about five times that of a national circuit over the same distance, and many user groups have stressed the deterrent effect of such cost differentials on the growth of international information exchange. In the special case of satellite communications, there appears to be a price factor of about eight.

To my knowledge, no one claims that international cooperation in information will bring lower costs for the system as a whole. It is interesting, for example, that in all of the early planning and design of EURONET (European Online Information Network), no public data on the economics of the system were available. Therefore, as purse strings tighten, it will become increasingly difficult to sell the idea of international cooperation, whether or not other aspects of the venture merit such an approach.

TECHNICAL FACTORS

The technology of today—communication systems, computer networks, facsimile transmission, and the like—provides more rapid and flexible means of information exchange than ever before. International time sharing networks such as MARK III and TYMNET provide the most extensive commercial networking operations in the world. Networks for scientific computing such as ARPANET (Advanced Research Project Agency Network) have been established as operational experiments. European networks for the distribution of scientific and technical information such as ESANET (European based information network operated by the European Space Agency), SCANNET (Nordic Network for Information and Documentation), and EURONET (European Online Information Network) are examples of planned or operating international systems.

It is clear that sufficient equipment and technology are currently available to handle all observed requirements for processing scientific and technical information. To be sure, there are gaps in the uniformity of equipment and some procedures, but, by and large, the barriers to international cooperation are not technological.

CONCLUSIONS

The future of AGRIS or of any similar system for agriculture appears bleak. It is difficult to imagine less favorable conditions for such developments at this time. Apart from the great technical sophistication that already exists, the preponderance of political, social, and economic factors militates against the successful operation of a worldwide system for agricultural bibliographic information.

The expressed information needs of any significant agricultural user group are too few, and the demands on limited resources by programs with higher priorities are too many, to permit the luxury of adequate trial operation of the service. These and other factors combine to produce a slowing in the planning and development of scientific and technical information systems in many countries. While UNESCO's UNISIST (Universal System for Information in Science and Technology) program supports the concept of strong, centralized national planning and unified information systems, there is little evidence that the concept is embraced in any practical way outside of the developing world and Eastern Europe.

Any successful international system for agricultural information in the next ten years must depend primarily on the United States and, in particular, on the National Agricultural Library. Thus, the future course will be determined by program decisions made at NAL and ultimately through programs approved and funded by the Congress.

The present ambiguities in policy and planning at the agency level make any forecast a guess at best. I, for one, hope and trust that NAL will provide whatever support to AGRIS is needed for as long as is necessary to determine the validity of the system concept and to protect the investment already made. Whatever actual trends occur, it seems certain that our future information society will exhibit new dimensions in each of its sectors. We must make sure that agriculture is served well.

NOTES

1. John McHale, *The Changing Information Environment* (Boulder, Colo.: Westview Press, 1976), p. 92.

2. Ervin Laszlo, *A Strategy for the Future* (New York: George Braziller, 1974), p. 53.

3. John Sherrod, "Automation in the National Agricultural Library," *Actas y Trabajos de la Segunda Reunion Interamericana de Bibliotecarios y Documentalistas Agricolas*, Bogotá, 2-7 Diciembre 1968. p. V-F-2. Bogotá: AIBDA.

4. Richard A. Farley, remarks appearing in Hearings Before a Subcommittee of the Committee on Appropriations, House of Representatives, Part 3, Agricultural Programs, 1977, p. 194.

5. William Knox, paper presented at the Special Session on Federal Information Policies, 40th Annual Meeting, American Society for Information Science, Chicago, Illinois, September 29, 1977.

6. Raymond Aubrac, "Information Science and Food in the Developing Countries," *Bulletin of the American Society for Information Science* 3, 3 (1977): 19-20.

7. U.S. Department of Commerce, Office of Telecommunications. *The Information Economy: Definition and Measurement* (Washington, D.C.: U. S. Government Printing Office, 1977).

8. Alex Tomberg, "On-Line Services in Europe," *On-Line Review* 1, 3 (1977): 177-193.

9. U. S. National Science Foundation, *Statistical Indicators of Scientific and Technical Communication 1960-1980, A Summary Report*, Volume 1. (Washington, D.C.: U. S. Government Printing Office, 1976).

10. Audrey Clayton and Norman Nisenoff, *A Forecast of Technology for the Scientific and Technical Information Communities*, Volume 1 (Arlington, Va.: Forecasting International Ltd., 1976).

11. International Institute for Applied Systems Analysis, *Study of the Potential Use of Informatics Technology on Problems of Scientific and Technological Cooperation* (Laxenburg, Austria: IIASA, 1977).

International Frontiers in Agricultural Information Services

DONALD LEATHERDALE*

We, involved in the field of agricultural documentation and
information, are as guilty as the followers of any other discipline of adding needlessly to the vast accretion of publications—publications which we ourselves at times rail against.
(If I may be allowed to digress after only one-and-a-half
sentences, it is my totally unsubstantiated belief that what
we are all up against is not so much an "information explosion"
as a "publication explosion." These two terms are by no means
synonymous. I hope to return to this point later, when it will
no longer be a digression.)

Be that as it may, when I was invited to present a paper on
"International Frontiers in Agricultural Information Services"
(albeit changed, I must admit, at my own request, from "International Frontiers in Agricultural Librarianship"), the first
question I asked myself was: "What can I say that will not be
condemned as yet another addition to that rapidly growing pile
of documentation on agricultural documentation?" Even four
long years ago, when Jacques Tocatlian was preparing his review of international information systems,[1] he was able to say

*Donald Leatherdale is in the Information Sciences Division,
International Development Research Centre, Ottawa, Canada.

that the documentation on just one system, AGRIS, was volu-
minous.

So, as our starting point for looking at some of the aspects
implied by the "international frontiers" of the title, let us take
the year 1975. In that year, not only was Tocatlian's paper
published, but also there were other landmark publications concerning agricultural information in the world picture. Philippe
Ariès took the development of agricultural information services
in the world as the theme for his presidential address to the
Mexican Congress of the International Association of Agricultural Librarians and Documentalists.[2] The proceedings of a
symposium on international information exchange, jointly
sponsored by the Food and Agriculture Organization (FAO),
the International Atomic Energy Agency, and UNESCO,[3] were
published, and AGRIS moved into an operational phase to
begin the on-going publication of *AGRINDEX*.

Viewed from the international viewpoint, agricultural information covers many things and involves many different
types of services, catering to a wide range of users. We all
remember two compilations of data on such services, both issued before 1975: von Frauendorfer's survey of 1969[4] and
Boyle and Buntrock's survey of 1973.[5] These surveys made us
all aware of the number of services available and of the great
differences between them: differences in scope, in the types
of user, in funding and organizational structure, in output
products, in language, in depth of treatment—in short, differences in any area one cares to mention. And yet, and this
must not be understated, the great majority of those services
were fulfilling a need.

It is almost axiomatic that the main use of agricultural information is to provide more and better food for mankind.
Whether one is a phytopathologist attempting to elucidate
the physiology of resistance to a disease in maize, a rural econ-
omist concerned with raising the living standards of migratory
workers, or a dairy farmer worried about increasing milk production from his herd because he wants a corresponding increase
in income, the fundamental information requirement is the
same. It has become fashionable to speak of "mission-oriented

systems," and in the case of agricultural information systems
the mission is, in the broadest sense, staring us in the face.

Is that enough? It could be thought to be enough were it
not for one hard fact that continues to creep into the picture.
It is one thing to list information in well-conceived classifica-
tions, to gather together as much information as possible, and
even to make it more useful by providing abstracts in a variety
of languages. But what if the people who would most profit
from that knowledge are still unable to get at these sources?
The barriers do not follow a common pattern. In one country,
the barrier to access may be a financial one—the information
may be acquired by a hard-currency payment, but hard cur-
rency just is not obtainable. A researcher in another country
may face the language barrier—he knows of the existence of
a very pertinent paper, but it is written in a language that he
does not understand. Perhaps the most common barrier is that
raised by the inaccessibility of documents. How frustrating it
is to be notified of a paper that would appear to be of the greatest interest, and yet not to be able to locate a copy of it. A different type of obstacle is that of comprehension—relevant
literature exists, but the potential user lacks the understanding
to appreciate it. Scientific history is full of instances of this
barrier, but away from the academic level we have the greater
problem of transferring information from the researcher to the
planner, the extension worker, the farmer.

These and other barriers are not necessarily insurmountable,
but they do gravely hinder the flow of information, particularly
in the international context and even more particularly in the
developing countries. Most systems that lay any claim to providing an international service are actively looking into how these
hardships may be alleviated. AGRIS should take a lead in remov-
ing these frustrations, for a system based within an agency of
the United Nations could be in a more advantageous position
than many others to take the appropriate actions. The International Nuclear Information System (INIS), for example, operating from the International Atomic Energy Agency, micro-
copies the full texts of nonconventional documents reported
to the system and makes these available on demand. The AGRIS

coordinating center, acting on feedback from national and regional centers, is investigating the organization of a service of that type. From its beginning, however, it has insisted that when a nonconventional document is entered into the system, the citation must be accompanied by a statement indicating where a copy of the full text may be obtained.

Access to conventionally published material, of which journal articles form the greater part, is assisted by many services (such as the Commonwealth Agricultural Bureaux [CAB] and the *Bibliography of Agriculture* in conjunction with the National Agricultural Library), but here again the question of hard currencies sometimes presents problems, despite the UNESCO-coupon scheme.

One step towards improving this kind of situation was taken by FAO in the setting up of AGLINET (the International Agricultural Libraries Network), whereby at present seventeen agricultural libraries of major importance in the various regions of the world (including the National Agricultural Library as the only member so far in North America) provide an interlibrary loan and copy service. AGLINET still has a long way to go, and one step is now being taken in the compilation of a union list of serial holdings. Much will depend on FAO for the successful operation of AGLINET, but, ultimately, (as with most international undertakings) the value of this system will depend on the active cooperation of its constituent libraries. Meanwhile, libraries in many surprisingly out-of-the-way places in the world rely, to a considerable extent, on the copy services of the British Lending Library.

So far we have considered some of the barriers that exist to getting hold of known documents, known information. How does the world stand concerning access to unknown information? I do not want to go too far back into even the recent past, but I guess it can bear repeating in the present context that the idea of AGRIS began to take form in 1969, when it was realized that the two main agricultural data sources—the National Agricultural Library with its CAIN (CAtaloging-INdexing) tapes and the *Bibliography of Agriculture*, and the Commonwealth Agricultural Bureaux with their series of specialized abstract journals—not only had a wasteful degree of overlap between them but, more important, were missing much pertinent documentation. The heads of these services at that time, John Sherrod[6] and Sir Thomas Scrivenor, respectively, approached FAO with their problems, since the FAO constitution declares that the collection, analysis, and dissemination of information relating to nutrition, food, and agriculture is one of the cornerstones of that UN agency. From these approaches emerged AGRIS, the early stages of which were succinctly described by the late Herbert Coblans.[7] The director-general of FAO nominated a panel of experts to advise him. It first met under the chairmanship of Sir Thomas Scrivenor and, later, under that of John Woolston, director of the Information Sciences Division of the International Development Research Centre (IDRC).

The system was designed as a decentralized operation, with each country undertaking the responsibility for inputting its own agricultural documentation. In this aspect, as in many others, AGRIS adhered to the successful pattern earlier established by INIS. Decentralization has several benefits. First, such a territorial formula virtually eliminates any possibility of duplication. Each country only inputs material issued in that country. Second, information is usually available more promptly in its country of publication than elsewhere. Indeed, I am not exaggerating when I say that many nonconventional documents will only be found by someone working within the national institutions. Third, translation into English (the carrier-language of AGRIS) is perhaps easier and cheaper when it is done only once and without the need for a polyglot team. Fourth, and I think most important, this type of system directly involves all the partners, which is a very healthy exercise. The number of countries cooperating continues to increase, and, correspondingly, output requirements are being more forcibly voiced.

Systems of the INIS-AGRIS type, transcending national frontiers, are naturally subject to many pressures, but let us not assume that these pressures are necessarily injurious. Perhaps the strongest pressure is the political one. That pressure was directly responsible for the establishment of INIS, but in the agricultural field, decision-making becomes diluted because of the many and diverse interests involved. John Woolston has described something of the process, as well as something of the qualms that existing services quite naturally have when faced with a healthy newcomer.[8] Political pressures, however, are not constant in their direction, and it is in this area that the virtues of linking international information endeavors with the political forum of international agencies become most apparent. The information needs of the developing countries have not, until recently, had political impact. However, we are now witnessing a fundamental change in this respect as the themes of the New International Economic Order assume reality. Woolston has looked a little way into the future:

> *From each according to his wealth, to each according to his needs*—this is the INIS-AGRIS formula, where *wealth* is measured by a country's production of information and *needs* are measured by its requirements for information. The rich countries are not seeking to retain a monopoly of knowledge and then exploit it to widen still further the gap between themselves and the Poor. But will the Poor believe that? Only if the Rich demonstrate a willingness to put their knowledge in the pool.[9]

The rich are indeed showing this willingness. For instance, while European Communities together supply the largest volume of input to AGRIS, Japan is inputting almost 100 percent of its agricultural information; Richard Farley[10] and the U.S. Secretary of Agriculture, Bob Bergland,[11] have indicated their belief that the United States must match this performance. As might be expected, national attitudes towards AGRIS have been extremely varied, ranging from all-out commitment to no response at all. After all, it is asking a lot of countries, particularly those with long-established and proven agricultural information services, to change to a new system that has yet to prove its worth. Arguments concerning the good of the world as a whole, the advantages of following UNISIST recommendations, and so forth, carry little weight under the circumstances.

This month, November 1977, will hopefully see a basic change in the attitudes towards AGRIS. A system designed on such a challenging scale invites caution while its future remains uncertain. That future will be decided upon at the Nineteenth FAO Conference Session this month. Evaluation studies of AGRIS have been carried out, and the results published in time for consideration by the conference members. It may be said that the system is still too young to be evaluated, but a spirit of cooperation is alive in the world, and the international agricultural information community would be irresponsible not to take advantage of it for the sake of the future of mankind. I remember being very impressed a few years ago when the AGRIS regional center for Southeast Asia, located at the Southeast Asian Regional Center for Graduate Study and Research in Agriculture (SEARCA), was being organized for continued operation. The director of SEARCA, J.D. Drilon, said that the region had such a need for inventories of its agricultural documentation and means of access to it that, even if AGRIS as a world system failed, the Southeast Asian component would "go it alone."[12]

FAO formally invited UNESCO to arrange for the independent evaluation of AGRIS. UNESCO's responsibilities were to establish terms of reference for the appraisal, to ensure that the UNISIST principles concerning international information transfer were adhered to, and to designate the members of the evaluation team. The appointed team consisted of two information-system specialists—F.W. Lancaster of the University of Illinois School of Library Science and John Martyn of the Association of Special Libraries and Information Bureaus (ASLIB) in the United Kingdom—and two agricultural experts—Osman Badran of the University of Alexandria, Egypt, and Janusz Haman of the Polish Academy of Sciences. As their report is available,[13] I do not propose going into the details of it here, although it might be useful to summarize the team's final recommendations. They endorsed the AGRIS concept and recommended as a top priority that FAO and other interested organizations should commit resources for the on-going operation and the development of the system. Another top priority was accorded to the need, "failing a more complete commitment of resources on the part of the United States," to develop a program for the transformation of NAL formats to those approved by the International Organization for Standardization. It was stated that full input of U.S. documentation was essential to the survival of AGRIS.

As secondary priorities, the team recommended the following: that increasing attention be devoted to the provision of output and services in exploiting the data base; that communication among the AGRIS centers and between them and the AGRIS coordinating center be improved; that a more aggressive approach be made to the promotion of the data base on magnetic tape and in the printed form of *AGRINDEX*; and that meetings of national liaison officers be arranged on a regular basis. Other recommendations included the need for a refined approach to indexing and information retrieval, for incorporating multilingual-access devices, for developing a subsystem for the supply of documents, and for continued monitoring of input quantitatively and qualitatively.

Following receipt of this evaluation report, the director-general of FAO is proposing to the FAO conference that the central coordination of AGRIS, its central processing and maintenance, and the costs of some development be included in the agency's regular program of work and budget for 1978-1979. He is also pointing out that the full implementation of the evaluation team's recommendations, the need for which he agrees, will only be achieved with the cooperation of, and provision of external resources by, other organizations.

Earlier, I referred to "evaluation studies" of AGRIS rather than to "an evaluation study." Concurrent with the evaluation arranged by UNESCO, the Agricultural Working Group of the European Communities requested a somewhat different type of evaluation. It was conducted by the German Centre for Agricultural Documentation and Information (ZADI) in Bonn and the Dutch Centre for Agricultural Publishing and Documentation (PUDOC) in Wageningen; essentially, it compared the values of the CAIN and AGRIS magnetic tapes to the user. (Incidentally, how often we fall into error here. There is always talk of considering users' needs in the design and development of an information system, but so seldom are those users meaningfully consulted. Of all the advice proffered during the design stage of AGRIS, some of the most pertinent derived from a meeting convened in Rome by the IDRC and FAO which brought together an important group of users of agricultural information from eleven less developed countries.[14]) I under stand that in the European Communities' evaluation, a comparison was made between the two tapes with regard to coverage, scope, and timeliness. I have been informed that the evaluation indicated that in all the parameters examined there was near equality between CAIN and AGRIS. This equality is all the more remarkable considering that the performance of an established system was being compared with that of a youngster— a system whose data base was only two years old.

Although the AGRIS and AGRICOLA (AGRICulture OnLine Access) tapes are searchable in a variety of ways, they contain little more than references to all documents. Their printed products, *AGRINDEX* and the *Bibliography of Agriculture*, are similarly restricted in their information contents. The subject content of the items cited may be broadly determined from their placement within categories in either system. Somewhat finer subject control for retrieval is provided in the *Bibliography of Agriculture* by a subject index using words derived from titles and title enrichment, and in *AGRINDEX* by a commodities index derived from coding selected at input. Both methods have been criticized, and no doubt will be improved from time to time. Nevertheless, neither system was designed to provide deeper selection. There are services that provide detailed abstracts and that select material qualitatively, rejecting much that is ephemeral or poor in intellectual quality. I need not describe such services to the present audience, but I will exemplify them by the Commonwealth Agricultural Bureaux (CAB) which, so far as they go, provide English-language services second to none in the world. The selection of worthy material from the unselected mass is a primary role of more selective services. It is to be hoped that the AGRIS data base will also provide them with the fullest coverage to ease their selection burden. Much that is being published today scarcely warrants being called "information" for it is repetitive, trivial, and often third rate. A decentralized system such as AGRIS will inevitably collect the bad with the good, despite guideline advice on identifying documents that should not be input. In so doing, however, it provides access to valuable information that has in the past been missed altogether.

The abstracting and information-packaging services with which we are familiar are themselves undergoing change, as are some of the patterns of agricultural research. Such changes should be reflected in the arena of agricultural information services as a whole. To take the example of CAB once again, the diverse approaches of its constituent institutes and bureaus are now mechanized and becoming standardized, which makes the CAB data base more flexible in operation. One spinoff is the production of abstract journals on specific topics, culled from their primarily discipline-oriented main series of abstract journals. An extension of this sort of activity is the establishment of information centers concerned with individual crops, groups of crops, or processes. These information centers not only possibly gather together abstracts of the literature on their specialty but also take the information process considerably further. The Cassava Information Centre, located at the Centro Internacional de Agricultura Tropical (CIAT) in Colombia, is a case in point. A bold attempt has been made to gather together as complete a collection as possible of the documentation on cassava, a crop of significant potential in the tropics that has been neglected for years. The retrospective material is abstracted, as are current additions, and the abstracts are published in book form and also distributed on cards to a worldwide network of specialists. Subject access to the whole collection is provided by an optical coincidence indexing system based on a thesaurus compiled for the purpose,[15] so that inquiries may be answered speedily. The center issues a semiannual newsletter of topical interest, a directory of workers on cassava-related problems, and a polished series of manuals which are of value not only to the researcher but also to the extension agent.

The Cassava Information Centre, as I have said, is located within CIAT, which is itself a manifestation of the new approach to research. The role of CIAT, one of the eleven research centers set up under the auspices of the Consultative Group for International Agricultural Research (CGIAR), is to foster agricultural development in the lowland tropics. One area of its expertise is tropical root crops, with outreach programs in many parts of the developing world. Many of the Consultative Group centers have good library facilities. Accordingly, the establishment of specialized information centers in such an environment means that the information center has access not only to the relevant documents but also to the expert knowledge of researchers. Thus, research teams participate in the information function and all parties benefit. I do not want to leave you with the impression that specialized centers are necessarily best located within institutions of the CGIAR, but they are best located in centers of recognized excellence.

The work of such specialized centers cuts across national boundaries, engendering reciprocal efforts around the world. Aware of the advantages of using computer-assisted systems, they and AGRIS regional centers are forging ahead towards the integrated use of fully compatible data bases. The process is most obvious in Europe, Latin America, and Southeast Asia, but it is to be hoped that other regions of the world will not be slow in realizing the potential benefits of full cooperation in these allied activities of agricultural information.

NOTES

1. Jacques Tocatlian, "International Information Systems," *Advances in Librarianship* 5 (1975): 1-60.

2. Ph. Ariès, "Evolution of Agricultural Information Services in the World: General Trends and the Present Situation," *Quarterly Bulletin IAALD* 20, 3/4 (1975): 105-110.

3. International Atomic Energy Agency, "Information Systems: Their Interconnection and Compatibility," in *Proceedings* of a symposium held in Varna, Bulgaria, 30 September-3 October 1974 (STI/PUB/379, Vienna, 1975).

4. S. von Frauendorfer, *Survey of Abstracting Services and Current Bibliographical Tools in Agriculture, Forestry, Fisheries, Nutrition, Veterinary Medicine and Related Subjects* (München: BLV Verlagsgesellschaft, 1969).

5. P. J. Boyle and H. Buntrock, *Survey of the World Agricultural Documentation Services.* Prepared on behalf of the FAO Panel of Experts on AGRIS (International Information System for the Agricultural Sciences and Technology) and of the Working Group for Agricultural Documentation and Information of the European Communities. FAO/DC/AGRIS 6 and EUR 4680/1e. (Rome: Documentation Centre, FAO, 1973).

6. John Sherrod, "The Role of NAL in the Developing World Information Systems," in *Actas y Trabajos de la Tercera Reunion Interamericana de Bibliotecarios y Documentalistas Agricolas,* Buenos Aires, 10-14 abril 1972, pp. III-B-2: 1-11 (Buenos Aires: AIBDA, 1972).

7. Herbert Coblans, *Librarianship and Documentation: An International Perspective* (London: Andre Deutsch, 1974).

8. John Woolston, "Sharing Knowledge: A Key to Detente between the Rich and the Poor," *Focus: Technical Cooperation* 4 (1976): 3-6.

9. Ibid., p. 6.

10. Richard A. Farley, "International Information Systems: Practical Reality," *Bulletin of the American Society for Information Science* 3, 3 (1977): 13-14.

11. Bob Bergland, "The World Food Situation," *Bulletin of the American Society for Information Science* 3, 3 (1977): 3.

12. J. D. Drilon, Jr., in *Proceedings* of a Workshop/Seminar on Regional Cooperation in Agricultural Information, held at College, Laguna, Philippines, March 3-12, 1975 (College, Philippines: SEARCA, 1975): 229-235.

13. O. A. Badran, J. Haman, F. W. Lancaster, and J. Martyn, *UNISIST Report on the Independent Appraisal of AGRIS Organized by UNESCO, November 1976-March 1977, at the Request of the Food and Agriculture Organization of the United Nations.* SC/77/WS/20. (Paris: UNESCO, 1977).

14. International Development Research Centre, *AGRIS and the Developing Countries.* IDRC-025e, f, s. (Ottawa: IDRC, 1974).

15. Donald Leatherdale, *Cassava Thesaurus* (Cali: Cassava Information Centre, CIAT, 1974).

National and International Research Centers: Their Contribution to Man's Survival in Our Time

May I first express my gratitude to those concerned for the invitation to contribute to this seminar, particularly as it is associated with a much respected colleague and friend, Foster Mohrhardt, with whom it has been my privilege and pleasure to work closely in the formative years of IAALD (the International Association of Agricultural Librarians and Documentalists)—virtually his term of office at the National Agricultural Library.

As a "civil servant," I must also make it quite clear at an early stage that the views expressed in this paper are entirely my own and are not to be regarded as those of my governmental department.

In this paper, I am proposing to consider largely the last thirty or so years when a great deal of reconstruction, rehabilitation, and change has affected virtually the whole world. On such a scale it was probably the last major occasion when swords were converted into ploughshares and more people of many nationalities sought and accepted independence. Agriculture, being a

*Frank C. Hirst is Chief Librarian, Ministry of Agriculture, Fisheries and Food, London. Paper was read by Carol Johnson, Chief, Analysis Division, National Agricultural Library.

very basic industry, had, of course, seen it all before; in Western civilization at least, one of our ideals, continuing improvement in the standards of life, is based on a pastoral text. Long after the times of subsistence farming, the church has continued to be a national and international force in development in this subject field.

The times when personal efforts and financial backing initiated agricultural research and development—the forward-looking farmers, growers, and breeders—gradually gave way to state support and the more widespread efforts of the industrial foundations. In many cases, however, these new sources of financial support were built on the foundations laid down by the earlier developers. Certainly in my own experience in the United Kingdom this applies. For instance, the Rothamsted Experimental Station which was founded on a family fertilizer industrial success gradually received increasing support from government funding—the Agricultural Research Council. I suggest that a similar pattern of development occurred in Europe, the United States, and most other countries. Your own Department of Agriculture not long ago celebrated its centenary; it has long been in the van of research and development in all aspects of agricultural production and marketing. In your country, such organizations as the Rockefeller and Ford Foundations have complemented the work of the state programs and have set up international centers and projects which are heavily dependent on the earlier efforts and cumulative expertise of federal and associated well-developed agricultural, educational, and research programs. In Canada, the International Development and Research Centre (IDRC) has a similar mission.

The most outstanding and far-reaching development in our time was surely the establishment of FAO (the Food and Agriculture Organization of the United Nations), originally based here in Washington. This organization also leaned heavily on what had gone before in the areas of research and development—particularly in the library, documentation, and publication field—when it moved to Rome where the library of the International Institute of Agriculture (associated with the earlier activities of the League of Nations) became the nucleus of its collections.

I am not proposing to consider in detail the work of individual centers, nor to compile a catalog by naming names. I don't think this is what the organizers of this symposium have in mind. As good practicing librarians, documentalists, and the like, we know full well the reference sources of information on on-going and past research from the reports of individual research stations and such titles as the *Experiment Station Record, Index of Agriculture and Food Research*, the *Bibliography of Agriculture, Agricultural and Biological Index* through the *Science Citation Index* and *WIPIS (Who Is Publishing in Science?)*, to name only some printed sources. It would seem more pertinent to survey major fields of interest and activity in the time available.

One major target of research has been improved performance—in crops and animals—linked closely with the local requirements of the grower, producer, and consumer. Rightly or wrongly, one lasting memory I have of an earlier visit to Beltsville is the development of the fourteen pound turkey largely with the typical New York or urban dweller in mind. Doubtless, in New Amsterdam the Dutch ovens coped with a full-size bird, and probably half a pig, at due season. More seriously, the aims were to breed in desirable qualities—bigger yields with less effort as disease resistance was developed on a selective basis. Less desirable qualities were similarly eliminated; in cereals, it was the weak, long stalks with susceptibilities to lodging. The sturdy short-stalk variety was found to be much more convenient to grow, harvest, and store. Hybrid maize is, I believe, the classic example of outstanding development in the North American continent with far-reaching benefits to mankind, equaled or perhaps surpassed only by the rice crop developments. Livestock improvement followed a similar pattern—bigger and better, and quicker to reach maturity: dual purpose cattle for economic milk and beef production—less fat and more lean; less butterfat in milk and dairy products; more manageable livestock (polled varieties of cattle, for instance) as herds became larger; breeds adaptable to varying climatic conditions and to microclimate environments as intensive cattle, pig, and poultry enterprises developed, to meet increasing demand at minimal cost.

In both animal and crop research, production for the convenience food market has received considerable attention in our time, from the era of the Chicago stockyards and canneries to more recent developments in refrigeration and accelerated freeze-drying processes. Parallel research in food science, technology, and transportation has had an important influence on animal and crop research in the more restricted field of agriculture.

There has been similar research in husbandry techniques from rearing to cropping, in fertilizer development—its production and application—and in mechanization of all aspects from preparation of the soil, its drainage, crop sowing, husbandry, harvesting, drying, and storing. Automation in animal husbandry has had its share of R & D (Research and Development). In developed countries with long-established systems of agriculture, I would venture to suggest that man was carried away with the idea that large-scale production was the only way to success—bigger or biggest was best. Man has come to realize that this is not always the case and certainly that this principle is not universally applicable. Nowadays, in the United Kingdom at least, in considering improvements for the developing nations in mechanization, the reverse is true—intermediate technology is more the order of the day. The increasing tendency to set up research stations and projects in the locality or regions where the results are to be applied has produced more beneficial results more rapidly and more economically. In the current political climate, this is inevitably the pattern of the future; paternalism has given way to indigenous home production.

Important developments have taken place in the storage of produce, involving designs of stores which are cheap and easily built using traditional skills and common, locally available materials—e.g., bamboo reinforcement of concrete in place of expensive imported steel mesh. So, too, improved methods of storage have resulted in longer life of cassava—for instance, from a few days after harvest to a month or more in simple straw-lined clamps. Or the simple ensilage of materials such as fruit or fish wastes, requiring no special equipment, is cheaper than drying, for it copes with seasonal gluts and provides fodder for farm animals.

The other two major fields of R & D have been (1) pest and disease control in crop and animal production and storage, not only in agricultural research, but also in the industrial chemical laboratories of universities and industry, and (2) human, animal, and plant pathology and pharmacology. Probably because of these activities, in recent times the ecologists have raised the outcry that too little attention is being paid to deleterious side-effects of high-level agriculture. For Rachel Carson and her successors, maybe the time was ripe for a cautionary note to be sounded, but it is worth remembering that systematic agriculture itself is a violation of nature and the natural order of things—even at subsistence levels—and the more so as it attempts to meet the basic needs of a quite complex pattern of life.

And where does all this fit into the main theme of this symposium? The motto of FAO, as you probably know, is *Fiat panis.* But man does not live by bread alone, but by knowledge, information—its transfer, interpretation, and application—and this is really what concerns our professional activities. Research per se may have some value to the few, but it is the result of research which is communicated and transformed into development that produces the major benefit to the widest audience. In this field too, national and international organizations are playing their part. Man was finding himself swamped by increasing outpourings from R & D establishments and personnel; as more people engaged in these activities, an unprecedented increase in the volume of publications culminated in the information explosion. Like most explosions, it had widespread and varying effects—a fair amount of duplication and regurgitation and considerable variation in quality of the output. Information exploiters met these problems with more qualitative selection and utilized the techniques of miniaturization and mechanization to keep the situation under control. Your own project ABLE could but lead to product CAIN (CAtaloging-INdexing)—even if AGRICOLA (AGRIculture OnLine Access) has not perhaps broadened the field. An international, FAO-based, cooperative experiment in the effective exploitation and dissemination of information, AGRIS (International Information System for the Agricultural Sciences and Technology) is still looking for a bigger share of input to increase its effectiveness and world coverage. A related international abstracting service covering world literature and closely linked with agricultural research stations, the CAB (Commonwealth Agricultural Bureaux), is currently providing input for three nations' output and could usefully add to this; the input of the nine European Community countries is coordinated; other international research organizations are also cooperating, i.e., AIBA (Agricultural Information Bank for Asia) and IACADI (Inter-American Center for Agricultural Documentation and Information). From this North American continent, the IDRC has played a key role in initiating and developing this system and is continuing to support its further development and improvement.

A similar FAO program known as CARIS (Current Agricultural Research Information System) was begun in 1971 and has continued to disseminate information on the ever-growing agricultural research and development activities. Initially, a project was mounted covering the area of the West Africa Rice Development Association (WARDA) as typifying a variety of soils, climates, research stations, and locally important crops, and where two different languages (French and English) were involved in R & D work. This project has recently been evaluated. The overall results seem to indicate that computer technology has a part to play in such an activity and that printed directories of current research are needed and appreciated in developing countries as more and more indigenous R & D activities are undertaken.

In these many ways, research and development in basic agricultural techniques have, it is suggested, made a considerable contribution to man's survival, but this is a time neither for complacency nor for complete satisfaction with what has been accomplished. Given a world population of some four billion people, one half to one billion of whom are still chronically underfed, a great deal remains to be done. In the scientific and technological fields, R & D has increased significantly over the years; its application in extension or advisory services has also made considerable progress. In the developing countries, more research into local problems and advice on their solution using indigenous materials and appropriate technology are needed. "The bag of fertilizer to every native farmer syndrome" is prevalent in some circles, but the appropriateness of that fertilizer to local conditions, its economic availability, and its application in season and in quantity are factors which often seem to receive scant attention. Where the abundant local energy sources are manpower, water, and wind power, and not fossil fuels which have to be imported at inflated costs, it is the development of these sources which must be emphasized.

In the socioeconomic fields, R & D is much less well developed, but it is of great significance if world population and the available food resources are to be matched—better matched than they are at present. In the developing countries, the results of medical and nutritional research have increased longevity and the potential for improved human output. Much remains to be done locally to improve the basic quality of life to a stage beyond mere survival.

I have covered a number of topics which seem important to me in the theme of this paper. In a symposium of this kind, as I see it, a major purpose is to stimulate thought and broaden the theme by discussion.

NOTES

1. "The World's Need for Food . . . Can Information Help?" *Bulletin of the American Society for Information Science* 3, 3 (February 1977).

2. National Academy of Sciences, *World Food and Nutrition Study* (Washington, D.C., 1977).

3. P. Harrison, "Beyond the Green Revolution," *New Scientist* 74 (June 1977): 575-578.

Management in Agricultural Research Libraries: The Next Thirty Years

*WALLACE C. OLSEN**

As has often been noted, the task of prediction is an easy one since no one can possibly prove or disprove what is said. I would like to take a slightly different tack which might avoid that rather smug position. Predictions must be based on the actions of the present or the past. Therefore, I feel it is best to begin with a view of the major influences or trends affecting us. From these and historical and economic observations, perhaps some valid projections can be made. This symposium is concerned with the international arena, although my title does not so specify. I am unable to make predictions for agricultural research libraries throughout the world, but the trends and possible implications for libraries in the United States and many Western countries may allow for analogies.

INFLUENTIAL TRENDS

Not always, if ever, are we the masters of our fates. This is particularly true in public service institutions and has become

*Wallace C. Olsen is Deputy Director for Library Services, National Agricultural Library.

an accepted management fact of life in academic and federal libraries. When we are able to influence these factors, we are more so the pilots of our fates; then we will have become good managers and administrators, at least of our own perpetuation. My list of influencing trends includes those having both positive and negative sides.

1. *Centralization* of campus departmental libraries has been a trend for twenty years, if not longer. That consolidation is continuing, with many agricultural libraries becoming science libraries. With this centralization outside of departments or colleges of agriculture has come the inexorable reduction of services and the use of a collection by researchers, advanced students, and field practitioners. The barrier between the working professional agriculturalist and librarian seems much enlarged once merger with larger units takes place. This trend, which has several positive aspects, has also been detrimental in numerous institutions.

2. *Budget* squeezes hit the academic community hard beginning ten years ago; they have had a heavy impact in the federal community within the past five years. The reasons are as numerous as the leaves of Villombrosa: inflation; sometime low productivity and performance; fewer students, a fact which is reflected in many academic library budgets; inappropriate assessment of the library and its role in a modern, wired world; inability of library administrators to sell their programs; and just plain tired blood, to name a few. Clearly, agricultural research libraries in the United States are not maintaining the fiscal position they held a few years ago. It should be noted that increased funding to overcome some of these shortages may have been diverted to obtain the services from other sources. These fiscal pressures have another side—sharing responsibilities and cooperating become serious topics. This rarely happens in periods of affluence. But isn't that the position public institutions should be in?

3. *Decision-making* in libraries has moved farther down the ladder to lower administrative levels, often with traumatic experiences. The resulting adjustments in viewpoint, approach, and relationships should produce a more positive attitude, provided the horse isn't killed on the way to the gate. This

manner of managing is critical to librarianship if we are to come
out from under the weight of daily routines, create fully competent professionals able to operate at top administrative levels,
and increase quality and productivity through innovation, planning, and imagination. Not all of us have succeeded in instill-
ing professional and forward-looking managerial points of view.
As the number of professionals for interaction with the public
becomes fewer, the demand for level-headed, alert decision-
makers at lower levels becomes imperative.

4. *Information as a utility* is a popular concept today. Information in this context includes the contents of books, on-
line bibliographic files, or numerical data bases retrievable
by computer. The United States and most Western European
nations are rapidly moving into the postindustrial period. Information as a marketable commodity with the usual owner-
ship guarantees has clearly grown as a part of the gross national
product. We are swinging from the exportation of tractors to
the sale of information, expertise, and knowledge by way of
consultants, surveys, analyses, and plans for technical and social
well-being. And the price is high. This trend, backed by commercial force, is very influential on the library community and
its direction. For a librarian, of course, this is no revelation
since we have long espoused the slogan "Knowledge Is Power."
However, the recent pace of commercialization has astounded
many of us.

5. *Automation* has begun to provide a way out of the maze
of high costs with low bibliographic output after fifteen years
of jerky starts and stops. The economics of computer handling,
the ease of learning alternative methods of processing, and the
dramatic potential for services and products have all made us
expectant of more and better things to come. These mechanical
slaves help perform many housekeeping and bibliographic
chores and are now operating *for* us, not *against* us, as was often
the case in the past. We can be very optimistic that increased
productivity through this and other technology will grow at a
faster rate than in the past few years.

6. *Human needs* for food around the world, as well as nutrition education here and overseas, are growing as the population
increases, as the natural resources diminish, and as the cost

per calorie goes up. Agriculture in the United States has now
attained a new level of respectability, social consciousness, and
commercial importance. So it is likewise throughout much of
the world. Agriculture is on an upward incline which is bumpy
with difficult social and technological questions. In the 1980s,
agriculture will share world concern with energy and within
the United States will be the new moon-shot syndrome. We are
part of that growth and concern and have an important role to
play. And we will be allowed to play, if we are up to it.

MANAGING THE FUTURE

While these six broad influences affecting agricultural research
libraries could be broken into subcategories and other influences
could be added, these are the primary factors we have seen or
will feel. The outside influences reflect the fact that we are not
living in a solitary world, although some of us would sometimes
like the quiet of it. To express this another way, managing the
future is not in *our* hands alone. But the will to go beyond what
we have attained and to strive toward improvement must be
within our managerial command. Without it, society will pass us
by.

This sermonette brings us back to basic elements of management: such mundane and essential items as personnel, money,
efficiency, bringing about needed changes, and doing it all effectively.

WHAT'S AHEAD

With this as background, I offer some observations about
managing agricultural research libraries in the next twenty-
five to thirty years. These won't be new or astounding, although
my emphases may be.

1. *Commercial services* in all aspects of agricultural information and bibliographic activities are going to grow in significance.
I can envision some information services, including electronic
delivery methods, so effective and low in cost that researchers
and students will have at-home services which will answer the

greater portion of their information needs. This change will force agricultural libraries to reassess their continuing responsibilities in a free enterprise system where information is a utility. In addition to the usual long-term archival chores and collection tasks now performed by libraries, there will be added new dimensions of services—services which cannot be accomplished in the economic marketplace. These services will concentrate on specialized contacts, sophisticated referrals to agricultural experts or joint work with them, creation of new and unusual bibliographic and information aids, mapping, and assisting in the implementation of information systems. Most of these services will be for the immediate organizational clientele.

2. *Labor-intensive* tasks will continue to disappear from our libraries when automation does not provide a way and the costs are high. These will go to places in the world where adequate intellectual sophistication exists and where the labor costs are substantially lower. Please don't misunderstand me; with automation and other mechanical techniques, we will continue *wherever possible* to hold onto products and tasks involving heavy labor investments. There is a strong American desire *not* to give up but, rather, to invent a better raft to keep people and their jobs afloat. Perhaps we will be able to do so in agricultural research libraries and in the commercial world from which many of our ideas for improvement come. But I am skeptical for the long term.

3. *Personnel* in agricultural research libraries will become more specialized in technical agriculture and closely allied sciences. If we wish to provide more sophisticated information and bibliographic services, specialization may become a requirement. It is clear from examples in this room that this need not be, since the librarian or information scientist who does a job well and can clearly explain and demonstrate results can also interact intelligently and beneficially with the agriculturalist without need of agricultural credentials. However, I believe these cases are too few to override the demands which will be made to get disciplined specialists into our organizations.

4. *Decentralized* library services seem a certainty to me whether in a campus setting or a large federal department. This

will not be a reversion to the departmental or college library pattern of the past, but a derivative of it. Having major collections with attendant service staff in numerous locations of an organization seems an economic impossibility even if it were desired. What seems to be evolving is a small collection library or information center where there is an adequate number of resident agriculturalists, with a small, highly concentrated book and journal collection, a responsive and well-trained staff, largely professional, hooked with a large backup agent for materials and assistance as needed. This unit would handle 75 percent or more of its inquiries on an immediate or one-day period and with competent responses. Housekeeping chores would be at a minimum and would be automated or shifted to the backup unit. Such libraries and information centers are now spotted around the federal establishment, the best examples probably being those serving the U.S. Congress. The shelflife of the librarians in such centers is relatively brief, so either we breed a new strain to handle the situation, or we rotate people in and out routinely. What we create is a barebones departmental or close-at-hand library with no permanent collection and a library which concentrates on staff in order to be highly responsive to expanding information needs.

5. *International* responsibilities are coming to agricultural research libraries in the United States because of the political funding processes and because we have knowledge and expertise which can be used elsewhere in the world. The land-grant community is spearheading this thrust, which is approaching rollercoaster momentum. To a large degree, the libraries and information services will ride along as one more instrument for technology transfer. I see this influence affecting hiring needs in many of the land-grant libraries, so that language skills, political acumen, and negotiating ability may become real, not imaginary, job requirements.

6. *Evaluations*, reexaminations, scientific management, and quantitative measurements must be an increasing part of the management scene in the next thirty years. Society is less willing

today to accept numbers games or backpatting exercises, but we will be asked to make intelligent examinations of what is happening in our libraries, as well as how we can best get to where we want to be and implement policies which befit public institutions. Such a manager must also be a leader, of course, and able to display the human value side of an organization, as well as its efficiency, intelligence, and know-how. This may be where many libraries in the United States lack talent. I reiterate, we had better get this factor into our management practices or the chickens may be stolen, along with the coop.

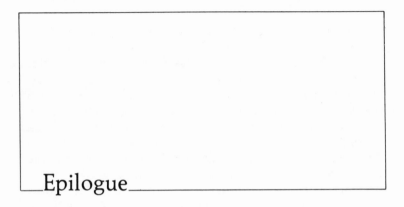

Epilogue

*JEANNE M. HOLMES**

This symposium has focused attention on the role of agricultural librarians and documentalists in the world war against hunger. With that theme in mind, the participants have provided abundant food for thought for some time to come.

To get to the point, though, this has been a day to remember. The presence and words of the speakers testify to the importance of agricultural library and information service in the world of today and of tomorrow. They have given due credit for accomplishments to date, but they have also, frankly and properly, pointed out shortcomings and tasks left undone, and they have suggested possible courses of action for the future.

There is a message in the fact that future action is proposed. Optimism and determination are not totally lacking, despite the awareness of problems already identified and those likely to catch us unaware and unprepared.

It would probably be fatuous to think, let alone to say, that the ideal international agricultural information system will spring full-blown from this symposium. It is not too much to

*Jeanne M. Holmes is Deputy Director for Resource Development, National Agricultural Library.

hope, however, that the speakers' messages will invite attention to the necessity for renewed efforts.

If those efforts are to be successful, there must be continuing communication—communication among machines, of course, but, most of all, true communication among people. It has been especially heartening to hear the acknowledgments today of the value of human contributions to international agricultural information services.

No one personifies those contributions to a greater degree than Foster Mohrhardt, who has furthered those services through his direction of programs of the National Agricultural Library and the Council on Library Resources. Certainly, the symposium was appropriately highlighted by the highly deserved tribute to this outstanding international agricultural librarian.

Index

ABOUT THE EDITORS

Alan Fusonie is historian and librarian with the U. S. Department of Agriculture, National Agricultural Library, and associate professor at the University of Maryland and Prince Georges Community College. He has had articles published in *East European Quarterly* and the *Quarterly Journal* of the International Association of Agricultural Librarians and Documentalists, and is currently working on a guide to manuscripts in the National Agricultural Library.

Leila Moran is chief of the Reference Branch, Technical Information Systems. She is the editor of the book *Heritage of American Agriculture.*